641.6374

D0274728

CHOCOLATE

CHOCOLATE

EASY RECIPES FROM TRUFFLES TO BAKES

Molly Bakes

Photography by
Georgia Glynn Smith

◙ SQUARE PEG

This book is for Farah who loves chocolate.
She loves to talk about it, she loves to eat it and now
hopefully she'll also learn to cook with it.

CONTENTS

INTRODUCTION

Chocolate. It has always been my weakness, along with cakes – and anything else that's sweet, for that matter.

I did more eating than baking until recent years. It's not that I didn't want to cook, it's just that I had been lucky enough to be surrounded all my life by parents and relatives who were great cooks, so I didn't feel the need to learn.

It all started with unemployment and boredom. I suddenly became interested in making food rather than just eating it. I wanted to make great cakes and had not much else to do than experiment in the kitchen. Baking quickly became my passion. It was 2009 and the start of the recession when, in my parent's North London kitchen, Molly Bakes was born.

I love cooking with chocolate and it has always been an important ingredient for me in the bakery. But I must admit I've felt daunted too, especially when it comes to tasks more complex than swirling chocolate through bakes. It needs to be melted carefully and then tempered if you want it to look perfect. Then there's all that dipping and moulding. It sounded like a great big faff.

Then one day I asked myself, 'Are you the same girl who started a baking business from nothing but enthusiasm?' Deep down I knew I was afraid of learning something again – so I gave myself a pep talk and haven't looked back.

While I am not going to call myself a chocolatier (that takes up to 5 years' study), through practice I've overcome my fear and now regularly experiment with different recipes to create chocolates for the Molly Bakes range. After all, chocolate and cake go so well together.

This book is for anyone who loves chocolate but wants easy and approachable recipes and techniques. You can make everything easily in your own kitchen, with very little equipment, from your own versions of childhood treats to boxes of chocolates as gifts.

Chocolate Origins

COCOA BEANS

The creation of chocolate – from bean to bar – is a fascinating and lengthy process. It's important to understand what goes into making this luxurious ingredient since there are so many varieties of chocolate available. Knowing how it is made will help you choose a good quality one. It's easy to be tempted to buy a cheaper alternative when there are so many on the market but I've always been a believer in using good quality ingredients. Remember, the higher quality the chocolate the better the recipes in this book will taste. I've given guidelines on how to choose the right chocolate on p.16.

Cocoa beans come from cacao pods which grow on the cacao tree, also known by its Latin name Theobroma cacao (meaning 'food of the gods'). This small, tropical tree originates in South and Central America but you can also find it growing in other parts of the world.

There are three main types of cocoa bean:

Criollo – The 'native' bean. This is the finest type of cacao or cocoa and the most expensive. Originally from Venezuela, it is also the rarest because criollo trees are less adaptable to different climates and today there are very few true criollo trees remaining. Criollo chocolate bars have a distinctive and complex taste which can include flavours of caramel, nuts, vanilla and tobacco.

Forastero – The 'foreign' bean. The most common variety of cocoa bean, the forastero has been cultivated for mass production and can be found all over the world. Forastero beans represent 80% of the world's cocoa production and are used for making everyday chocolate.

Trinitario – A hybrid between criollo and forastero, the trinitario tree originated in Trinidad. The trees were developed after a mysterious disease struck Trinidad's criollo trees in 1727, damaging the country's cocoa economy. To salvage cocoa production, forastero seeds were planted and cross-pollinated with the remaining criollo trees to make this new variety. The trinitario makes up 10–15% of the world's cocoa beans today and is most likely to be found in fine chocolates.

Harvesting and Processing

Most African beans are of the common forastero variety. Ghana and the Ivory Coast are the world's largest producers of cocoa beans, and cocoa grown in Latin America and the Caribbean is generally of the highest quality.

A single cacao tree can produce up to 2000 cocoa pods a year but this is enough for only about 1kg of chocolate. The pods are rigid and shaped like rugby balls. They mature throughout the year, and each pod produces 30–40 seeds. It's from these seeds that cocoa solids and cocoa butter are extracted. It takes six months for a single cacao pod to ripen. If you were to eat the seeds straight out of the pod they'd be very bitter, nothing like the end product.

Twice a year the pods are harvested then fermented and dried in the sun for a week. The beans are then graded and roasted at high temperatures to intensify the flavours. The higher the roasting temperature, the more bitter the beans become so more sugar must be added. Cheaper chocolates are made this way. Good quality chocolate is made from beans that are roasted for longer at lower temperatures.

Next, the outer shells are cracked, leaving the 'nibs', which are crushed pieces of the bean. Cocoa nibs are edible and really chocolatey but still very bitter. They can be eaten raw as a snack, used as an ingredient or for decoration.

To make chocolate, the cocoa nibs are ground into a thick paste called cocoa liquor. This liquor is bitter and not like the smooth, creamy chocolate we know and love. By adding sugar, cocoa butter, vanilla and milk, the liquor is finally transformed into chocolate. How much is added to the liquor will depend on whether it is to make dark or milk.

REFINING AND CONCHING

To give the chocolate its creamy, smooth texture, the mixture is run through a series of steel rollers. It will then be 'conched'. A conch is a machine that mixes and aerates the chocolate. More ingredients, such as cocoa butter and soy lecithin, are added at this stage to help create texture. Conching lasts a few hours for lower quality chocolates and at least six days for finer ones.

TEMPERING

The final stage in the bean-to-bar journey is tempering. All chocolate will go through the tempering process. It's a cycle of melting, cooling, then remelting it at precise temperatures to stabilise the crystals. If chocolate is not tempered these crystals will not hold together and will cause 'blooming' (white specks) in chocolate.

Tempering gives chocolate a lovely shine and a 'snap' when you bite or break it. For an explanation of how to temper chocolate, see p.26.

Sources of Chocolate

SINGLE ORIGIN
Much like wine and coffee, the taste of cocoa is affected by the region in which it is grown.

Some manufacturers use up to 12 types of cocoa in their recipes but there is a movement towards using single-origin and single-estate chocolate. This chocolate is made from beans grown in one particular area or plantation.

Here are some of the flavours you can find in single origin chocolates:

Madagascan
light citrus notes like tangerine

Venezuelan
red fruits like plums and dark cherries

Trindadian
spicy flavours such as cinnamon

Jamaican
fruity with subtle pineapple flavours

FAIRTRADE
Around 50 million people depend on the production of cocoa for their livelihood. 90% of cocoa is grown on small farms. Most cocoa growers receive just 6% of the retail price of a chocolate bar. Buying Fairtrade chocolate ensures farmers are given a fair deal for their cocoa.

Types of Chocolate

Dark (also known as plain chocolate)
This usually contains over 50% cocoa solids, with finer chocolates containing 70% or more. There is less milk, sugar and cocoa butter in dark chocolate than in other types.

Milk
This contains more milk, sugar and cocoa butter than dark chocolate and is usually 33–50% cocoa solids.

White
Technically this is not real chocolate as it doesn't contain any cocoa mass. It is made from cocoa butter, sugar, milk solids and vanilla.

Couverture
This is usually sold as callets, which are purpose-made chocolate chips, and used in chocolate making for dipping and coating. It has a higher cocoa butter content than other types of chocolate, making it easier to use, as it melts and spreads more readily. It is available as dark, milk and white. You will see the term couverture used in this book as that is mainly what chocolatiers use.

Baking chocolate
This is very bitter, with a higher cocoa solids content than usual, and is normally used for baking and cooking. Use it in ganache or for making chocolate buttercream.

Mass produced chocolate (also known as compound chocolate)
In general these products only contain up to 20% cocoa solids. Cocoa butter is replaced with saturated and vegetable fats as well as powdered milk and additives.

Cocoa powder
Cocoa butter, which is a fat, is removed from cocoa liquor to make a dry substance that is then ground into a powder. Cocoa powder can be used in baking, cooking and for rolling truffles in.

Which Chocolate to Choose?

With so many types of chocolate to choose from, it's easy to be confused by cocoa percentages.

Most bars of chocolate or bags of couverture state the percentage of cocoa solids on the packaging. Knowing which one to use in cooking or baking depends on the type of recipe you are making and, sometimes, personal preference.

Chocolate intended for eating by itself usually has a maximum of 75% cocoa solids as anything above that tends to be very bitter due to its low sugar content. Chocolate with a cocoa solids percentage of 85% or above is great for baking with as it will normally be used in a sweet recipe, where the sugar content is balanced out, and it will give your cakes and brownies a lovely rich flavour. For the baking recipes in this book where chocolate is used, I recommend you choose a chocolate with a minimum of 70% cocoa solids. The higher the cocoa solids, the richer and deeper the flavour of your bakes.

For any of the filled chocolates, truffles, slabs and in recipes where chocolate is used for coating you can choose between milk or dark chocolate. If the recipe calls for dark chocolate, try to use one that's between 60 and 70% cocoa solids as this will have a good balance of bitter and sweet. Milk chocolate usually has between 20 and 40% cocoa solids and as it contains much more sugar and milk than dark chocolate, it's perfect for chocolate recipes and coatings where more sweetness is required.

When choosing chocolate, look for a brand that contains cocoa butter rather then vegetable fat. You don't have to use the most expensive types but you will love the results if you choose the best your budget will allow for. The baking section of a large supermarket or speciality equipment store should stock good quality and well-priced versions. For my personal recommendations, see Suppliers on p.180.

Equipment

You can make beautiful and delicious chocolates with relatively inexpensive equipment. Much of it you might already have in your kitchen if you're a keen baker. Later on you could invest in a few simple tools such as dipping forks, scrapers and moulds, and perhaps even some specialist equipment if you get really serious.

Wooden spoons
Use for stirring chocolate while melting.

Heatproof bowls
For melting and tempering. Metal bowls are best as they distribute heat more evenly and help keep the chocolate in temper. Take care when handling – they get hot.

Scrapers
These are used for scraping excess chocolate when moulding. An angled palette knife can also be used.

Piping bags
Disposable ones are recommended for piping ganache and fillings.

Praline moulds
For making beautiful, filled chocolates. The best ones are rigid and made from polycarbonate, but silicone ones can also be used. See Suppliers on p.180.

Chocolate bar mould
You can make luxurious bars using a simple bar mould. Add dried fruit, nuts, cocoa nibs or fudge pieces for delicious textures.

Greaseproof or baking paper
Useful for piping ganache onto when making truffles.

Acetate sheets
You will need these if making the heart-shaped chocolate box cake on p.169 or chocolate lollies (see p.34). Chocolate sets onto acetate, making it easy to peel off, and gives a shiny finish.

Lollipop sticks
Small paper lollipop sticks are best for making the chocolate lollies on p.34.

Dipping fork
You can find dipping forks in various shapes. I find a three- or four-prong dipping fork easiest to work with.

Cook's thermometer
This is useful not only for tempering but also when making some of the recipes in this book such as caramels and marshmallows. A digital thermometer is best for accuracy. You can also buy spatulas with an inbuilt thermometer, which are very helpful when tempering.

(continues overleaf)

Mixing and whisking

Use simple spatulas and wooden spoons for mixing, wooden spoons for beating, whisks for whisking, and metal spoons for folding ingredients in. If you have them, then you can use electric mixers or whisks but they're not necessities.

Bain-marie

Not a necessity but a bain-marie for the home may be a worthwhile investment which will make tempering easier. The traditional method of a bowl of chocolate melting over a pan of hot water on the stove or hob works just as well. And although we don't use this method in our bakery, you can melt chocolate at short 30 second intervals in a microwave too.

Marble or slate slab

While chocolatiers use a frozen marble slab for tempering, we'll be using one for making chocolate fans (see Techniques, p.42). A slate slab is easier to find and does the job just as effectively.

Food grade gloves

Chocolate melts really easily when handled by warm hands so it's a good idea to wear thin disposable vinyl gloves. These are also useful when hand-rolling truffles.

STORING CHOCOLATES

Tempering chocolate will give your truffles and chocolates a longer shelf life. Store in a cool, dry place, away from sunlight. Never store chocolate in the fridge or freezer, as this could cause white specks to appear (blooming). All of the ganache recipes in this book contain cream that has been boiled to sterilise it. Both the sterilising method and encasing the ganache in chocolate helps it to last for several days at room temperature, stored in an airtight container.

TECHNIQUES

Tempering Chocolate

Tempering is a process which breaks down the crystals in chocolate by melting it to a certain temperature, then forming them back together by cooling the chocolate down again, before finally stabilising it by bringing the temperature back up a few degrees.

It may sound like a finicky process but once you get going it's a sheer delight to watch this delicious ingredient transform from dull pieces to a beautifully silky-smooth and shiny liquid. It will ensure your chocolates look stunning.

Untempered chocolate is grainy, matte and can bloom: the chocolate develops unattractive white specks caused by crystal formations. Properly tempered chocolate is shiny and has a lovely snap when you break or bite into it.

When it comes to tempering, the quality and type of chocolate you use is important. Couverture chocolate is best for making the recipes in this book (see Types of Chocolate on p.14) as it has a higher cocoa butter content and is designed for melting and dipping. Regular chocolate won't temper as well. The finish won't be as polished and the chocolates may crack or look waxy.

The traditional way to temper chocolate is to use a marble slab, but that's not something everyone has lying around. There are also machines which do the process for you, but unless you are planning on starting a chocolate-making business this is an expensive process, as the machines cost a few thousand pounds. The method I use is called 'seeding', and is quick, cheap and easy.

SEEDING

Seeding is the easiest tempering method for the home cook. You add unmelted chocolate callets (purpose-made chocolate chips) or finely chopped chocolate to already-melted chocolate to bring the temperature down.

Callets are small pieces of chocolate that are designed for melting. They are like chocolate chips in size but more flattened and symmetrical – almost like miniature buttons. Most couverture is sold in callet form. You can buy chocolate callets from specialist chocolate suppliers (see p.180)

Most of the Classic chocolate recipes in this book require 450g of chopped chocolate or callets. If using a bar it's best to chop it into small pieces so it will melt more evenly. You won't need all of the chocolate but it is best to have extra for ease of dipping and to maintain the temperature. Any unused chocolate can be remelted at a later date but must also be retempered.

However if you just want to have fun and aren't worried about your chocolates having a shop-perfect finish, then any of these recipes can be made with untempered melted chocolate.

How to Melt and Temper Chocolate

450g chocolate, chopped,
**   or callets**
Cook's thermometer

Place 300g of the chocolate in a heatproof bowl. Heat 5cm of water in a pan and place the bowl of chocolate over the top, ensuring the bottom of the bowl is not touching the water. Allow the chocolate to melt slowly until the temperature reaches:

45–50°C for dark chocolate
40–45°C for milk chocolate
40°C for white chocolate

As soon as the temperature is reached, remove the bowl from the heat. Add the 150g of unmelted chocolate into the melted chocolate. Stir the chocolate together until the temperature reaches:

28–29°C for dark chocolate
27–28°C for milk chocolate
26–27°C for white chocolate

This will take 5–7 minutes. It's important to keep stirring during this process, as getting as much air as possible into the chocolate will help cool it down quicker. You can place a small bowl of ice or cold water underneath the bowl of chocolate to help cool it down quicker.

Now you need to increase the temperature but only by a few degrees, so take care. Place the bowl of chocolate back over the pan on a low heat until the temperature reaches:

31–32°C for dark chocolate
29–30°C for milk chocolate
28–29°C for white chocolate

Now your chocolate is tempered and ready to use. When working with tempered chocolate it's best to keep it 'in temper', especially if you are not using it all in one go, for instance if you are making lots of different things or dipping. This means maintaining it between the last set of temperatures listed on the previous page. Placing a bowl of warm water underneath the chocolate keeps it warm and within the above temperature range. Keep a thermometer in the chocolate and if the temperature begins to drop, place the chocolate back on the heat for a few seconds. If it begins to get too warm, place it over a bowl of cold water.

If the chocolate does drop too low in temperature and begins to set, the tempering process will have to be started again from scratch. If you overheat the chocolate, don't worry; as long as it hasn't burnt you can let it cool down again to set, and then restart the tempering process.

TEMPERING TIPS
Take your time, rid yourself of distractions and keep all the tools you need within easy reach.

Make sure the room you are working in is not too cool or too warm.

Don't try to temper too much chocolate in one go – it can be overwhelming. Take care not to allow any steam or water into the bowl of chocolate as this will either cause the chocolate to seize or prevent correct tempering. Use a low heat to avoid over-steaming. It's also a good idea to keep some paper towels handy.

Although we don't use this method in our bakery, you can also use a microwave for melting the chocolate, taking care not to let it burn or overheat. Heat for 30–60 seconds at a time, taking the temperature at each interval. As it gets closer to the correct temperature take greater care and heat it for less time. If you make chocolates often enough, consider investing in a small bain-marie to minimize or prevent the risk of steam getting into the chocolate.

Moulded Chocolates

450g chocolate of your
   choice, chopped, or callets
Ganache or filling (eg. salted
   caramel) of your choice
   (see pp.48–58)

Baking paper
Ladle or large spoon
28-hole praline mould
Scraper
Large plastic bowl
Disposable piping bag

Melt and temper the chocolate, following the method on p.26.

Lay a sheet of baking paper on a work surface or table, ready to catch drips. Using a ladle or a large spoon, spoon the chocolate liberally into the praline mould. Scrape the spillover of chocolate off the top and sides of the mould. Tap the mould on the work surface to remove air bubbles. Turn the chocolate-filled mould upside down over a plastic bowl and allow the chocolate to pour out. When the pouring slows down, use a scraper or large palette knife to tap the side of the mould to make more chocolate pour out.

Once all of the excess chocolate has poured out of the mould it will leave a thin coating of chocolate around each cavity. Scrape the top of the mould clean with the scraper, working towards you, and set the mould aside for the chocolate to set.

Once the chocolate has set, transfer your ganache or filling to a piping bag, cut the end off and pipe into each cavity, filling them almost to the top. Leave to set.

To seal, pour a new layer of chocolate over the mould, scrape the mould again to remove the excess chocolate and tap the side to release any air bubbles. Scrape the top of the mould clean and set aside to set.

Once it's set, check that the chocolate has retracted from the mould. Turn the mould upside down and tap gently on the work surface so the chocolates fall out.

For decoration ideas, such as painting and colouring praline moulds, see p.41.

Dipped Chocolates

450g chocolate of your
    choice, chopped, or callets
Filling of your choice (see
    pp.59–64), firm and chilled
Decoration of your choice,
    e.g. sea salt, edible gold
    leaf, spices, candied nuts
    (optional)

3-prong dipping fork
Baking sheet lined with
    baking paper

Start with all your equipment ready and within easy reach. Cut your filling into squares or rectangles, or roll into balls, firm and chilled.

Melt and temper the chocolate, following the method on p.26.

Balance your first piece of filling on the 3-prong dipping fork and lower it into the bowl of chocolate. Use the dipping fork to submerge the filling fully in the chocolate, then immediately place the fork back underneath it and lift out of the chocolate.

At this point you need to remove the excess chocolate, so resist the temptation to tap the fork on the side of the bowl and, instead, touch the bottom of the dipped filling on the surface of the chocolate a few times. Gently scrape any remaining excess off the sides of the bowl.

Slide the dipped chocolate off the fork onto the lined baking sheet, and leave to set.

Repeat with the remainder of your filling pieces.
If you are decorating your chocolates it's best to do it while they are still wet. You have a few minutes before they set, so you can dip a few and then decorate all of them together. Sprinkle with sea salt, edible gold leaf, spices, candied nuts, or even just making a wave pattern with a fork looks attractive.

Hand-rolled Truffles

450g chocolate of your
   choice, chopped, or callets
Ganache filling of your choice
   (see pp.48–58)
Decorations of your choice,
   e.g. chopped nuts, cocoa
   powder, chocolate flakes,
   chocolate vermicelli
   sprinkles (optional)

Disposable piping bag
Baking sheet lined with
   baking paper
Vinyl gloves

Line a baking sheet with baking paper. Melt and temper the chocolate, following the method on p.26. However, for truffles finished with a decoration e.g. chopped nuts, the chocolate need not be tempered.

Transfer your chosen ganache into a piping bag and cut the end off. Pipe small balls of ganache onto the lined baking sheet, then place in the fridge to set. Once set, take one ball at a time and, wearing vinyl gloves, roll it in your hands to create a smooth round truffle. Put it back onto the sheet and then into the fridge to set.

Once the truffles are chilled and set, put on your vinyl gloves again and pour a small amount of tempered chocolate into your hand. Take a truffle and roll it in between your chocolate-covered hands. Place on the lined baking sheet to set. For a perfect finish give each truffle a second coating of chocolate and either leave it to set or roll it straight away in a decoration of your choice – try chopped nuts, cocoa powder, chocolate flakes or vermicelli sprinkles to complement each flavour.

NOTE
If you prefer to roll your truffles just once, then use 300g of chocolate rather than 450g.

Chocolate Lollies

300g chocolate of your
   choice, chopped, or callets
Decorations of your choice
   (optional)

Baking sheet lined with
   acetate or greaseproof
   paper
Disposable piping bag
Paper lollipop sticks

Line a baking sheet with a sheet of acetate. Melt and temper the chocolate, following the method on p.26.

Transfer the tempered chocolate into a piping bag, and make a 1cm incision into the end of the piping bag. Hold the piping bag in position over the acetate and, squeezing gently, let the chocolate pour out slowly. If you keep your hand steady enough the chocolate will pour out into a near-perfect circle. When your lolly is the right size (ours are approx. 7cm in diameter), move on and start piping the next circle. You have a few minutes before the chocolate sets so you can pipe a few before adding lollipop sticks and decorations.

Before the chocolate sets, insert a lollipop stick horizontally into each chocolate circle until it's halfway through, and twist it until the top half of the stick is completely covered and disappears into the chocolate. If decorating your lollies, do this now. Try sprinkling with popping candy, nuts, candied flower petals, dried fruit or even sweets such as mini marshmallows. Once the chocolate has set, you could drizzle with contrasting colours of chocolate.

NOTE
You can use this technique without the sticks to make the white chocolate wafer thins to decorate the Halloween mousse pots on p.174.

Piping with Chocolate

Chocolate is a wonderful substance to pipe with. If tempered correctly, it melts and sets hard so that you can pipe almost any shape and use as decorations to adorn cakes, desserts and truffles.

You can use a disposable piping bag fitted with a small round piping nozzle – a number 1.5 or 2 piping nozzle is usually best. However, you will get a better finish if you make a piping bag out of baking or parchment paper.

All you need is a large rectangle of baking paper and a pair of scissors.

Take the lower corner of the rectangle of paper and fold upwards so that it reaches the top edge of the paper. Run your finger along the fold to make a crease.

Fold it in again so the folded section is halved. Now roll the whole of the folded section into a cone shape, without creasing it. Put your hand inside the cone to open it out, trim off any excess paper with scissors. If you want to, you can secure the cone with a piece of tape.

Now you have your bag, fill it with tempered chocolate, referring to the detailed method on p.26, and cut a small hole to let the chocolate out.

Fold down the top of the piping bag. To pipe, gently squeeze the piping bag and apply an even pressure to pipe out your chosen design. Sometimes the chocolate at the tip starts to solidify so if this happens pinch it out through the hole with your fingers and continue piping.

It's best to pipe your designs onto acetate (but baking paper is also fine) and let them set completely before gently peeling back the acetate or paper to remove the decoration.

Flavouring Chocolate

Most chocolate comes already flavoured with vanilla that has been added by the manufacturer. However, you can buy flavouring oils for use in chocolate. These are available from specialty ingredients shops, cake craft shops and online (see Suppliers on p.180).

While ganache can be flavoured with alcohol and alcohol-based extracts, which are readily available in supermarkets, melted chocolate on its own cannot be flavoured with these as the water in them will cause the chocolate to seize – harden and clump.

Common oil-based flavourings for chocolate include mint, cherry, strawberry, hazelnut, cinnamon and orange. If you are making unfilled chocolates, such as lollies or plain moulded bars, then these flavourings can add a fun and unique taste.

Remember that oil-based flavourings are potent and should be used sparingly. They may be too overpowering and it's not necessary to use any when making filled chocolates.

Colouring Chocolate

You can colour white chocolate using powdered food colours or oil-based colourings, and this can be fun to do if you are planning to fill chocolates using novelty moulds.

As with flavouring, remember not to use any alcohol- or water-based colourings as these will cause the chocolate to seize.

When the chocolate is melted and tempered, add a colouring a little at a time and stir with a spatula until it is evenly incorporated. It's best to build up colour gradually to achieve the shade you want. Take care if using oil-based colourings as too much can alter the taste of the chocolate.

Painting Chocolate Moulds

Cocoa butter
Edible dusting powders
   of your choice

Selection of good quality
   paintbrushes
Praline mould

For an attractive finish on pralines, the moulds can be painted with cocoa butter or dusted with food colouring powders before they are filled with chocolate.

You can buy cocoa butter in various colours specifically for chocolate painting, but they can be expensive. The best I've found come from Squires Kitchen (see Suppliers on p.180), who sell them in small pots in sets of different colours, and it is relatively inexpensive to buy the sets. To use, just melt in a microwave or bain-marie according to the manufacturer's instructions.

To paint, take a fine artist's brush, dip it in the melted cocoa butter and paint dots, stripes, swirls, or anything you like, on the inside of each cavity of the praline mould before filling with chocolate. When you remove the chocolates, the paint will come off with them.

You can use the same technique to paint details into novelty chocolate moulds. You can also dust the praline moulds with food colouring powders. Metallic powders give a really high-end finish. Simply dust the cavities with the powders, using a soft paintbrush, before you fill with chocolate.

Chocolate Fans or Curls

A useful and fun technique to learn when starting out with chocolate making. Chocolate fans look impressive and are perfect for decorating cakes or desserts.

FOR THE FANS

300g dark, milk or white chocolate, chopped, or callets

Marble or slate slab, frozen
Palette knife
Vinyl gloves
Baking paper

FOR THE CURLS

300g dark, milk or white chocolate, chopped, or callets

Marble or slate slab, cold but not frozen
Sharp chopping knife or cheese plane

FOR THE FANS

When making these it's important to work quickly and only attempt to make one fan at a time.

Melt and temper the chocolate, following the method on p.26.

Pour a little of the tempered chocolate onto a frozen marble or slate slab and use a palette knife to spread it into a long rectangle. The chocolate will instantly start to harden but still be easily pliable.

Put on a pair of vinyl gloves and, working quickly, use your to hands create folds about 2.5cm wide from the base of the chocolate, until you have a fan shape. Place each fan on baking paper to prevent condensation forming, and leave to set.

FOR THE CURLS

Melt and temper the chocolate, following the method on p.26.

Pour all of the tempered chocolate onto a cold marble or slate slab, then use a palette knife to spread it evenly into a layer. Set aside in a cool place until just set but not solid.

Hold the knife or cheese plane and drag it towards you at an angle, scraping off a thin layer of chocolate into a curl as you go.

Chocolate Pudding Cups

This is a fun way of making edible dessert cups to fill with ice cream, brownies or other desserts – and it's easier than it looks. A great way to spend an afternoon if you're planning a party. These cups will keep well for several weeks if stored in an airtight container in a cool, dry place.

6 regular balloons
450g chocolate, dark, milk or
**   white, chopped, or callets**

Baking paper

Line a tray with baking paper and set aside. Blow up the balloons halfway to their full blown-up size. Gently wipe them with a damp cloth and let them dry. Melt and temper the chocolate, following the method on p.26.

Take one of the balloons and dip it in the tempered chocolate – dip it deep enough so that the chocolate forms a bowl around the balloon.

Remove it from the bowl of chocolate and place on the lined tray with the balloon tie facing up. Repeat with the remaining balloons.

Leave the chocolate to set, then simply remove the balloons from the set chocolate bowls – you can also burst them with a pin or sharp knife if you want to have some fun. Store until ready to serve. It's best not to put them in the fridge as the chocolate may bloom.

CLASSIC CHOCOLATES

Three Ways With Ganache

Ganache is a smooth chocolate paste, based on just two ingredients: chocolate and cream. It is much loved by chocolatiers for its myriad uses. Ganache with a firm consistency can be rolled into truffles, softer ganache makes a filling for chocolate or frosting for cupcakes, while at its most liquid it can be poured over a cake to form a chocolate ganache glaze.

200g dark chocolate, chopped, or callets
200ml double cream
20g unsalted butter, softened (if using as a glaze)

Place the chocolate in a medium-sized heatproof bowl and set aside.

Heat the cream in a small saucepan over a medium heat. If using butter to make a chocolate glaze ganache, heat it with the cream. Bring to the boil and immediately pour over the chocolate. Stir gently until smooth and all the chocolate has melted.

FOR A GLAZE
Allow the ganache to cool slightly before pouring over cakes as a glaze. The longer you allow the ganache to cool, the thicker it sets.

FOR A WHIPPED GANACHE
To make the ganache the right consistency for piping onto cupcakes, chill it for 30 minutes, then whip using an electric hand whisk or food mixer. You can pipe this onto cupcakes or into praline moulds for chocolates.

FOR TRUFFLES
Cover the bowl with cling film and refrigerate the ganache until firm. This can be done for several hours or overnight. For instructions on how to make truffles, see p.32.

FLAVOURING GANACHE
You can add alcohol, fruit purées, nuts, spices and other flavourings to ganache. The trick is to take care with liquid, for this recipe 1 tablespoon of alcohol or fruit purée is plenty. On the following pages I have included some flavoured ganache recipes to fill your chocolates with but why not experiment with your own combinations?

Salted Caramel Chocolates

I've always liked a little salt with my sweet. For as long as I remember, I've loved finding a few pieces of salty popcorn among a bucket of sweet at the cinema. In recent years, salt and sweet has become an on-trend flavour pairing but I think it's on its way to becoming a timeless classic.

GANACHE FILLING
85g unsalted butter
100g golden caster sugar
50ml golden syrup
125ml double cream
½ tsp fleur de sel or Maldon
   sea salt

COATING
450g milk chocolate,
   chopped, or callets

Cook's thermometer
28-hole praline mould

Makes 28

FOR THE GANACHE FILLING

Melt 70g of the butter and all of the sugar and golden syrup together in a heavy-bottomed pan over a medium to high heat. Leave to simmer for 2 minutes until the butter has melted, stirring gently every now and then.

Once the butter has almost melted, stir the sugar continuously with a wooden spoon to break it up. If the sugar clumps together just keep stirring, it will melt. Pay close attention so it doesn't burn, making sure you move all of the sugar around the pan especially around the centre and sides.

Continue cooking until the mixture reaches a deep amber colour. At this point it can burn easily so keep a close eye on it. Use a thermometer and get the temperature up to 176°C. Immediately add the rest of the butter and stir gently until melted.

Remove from the heat and slowly pour in the cream. Stir until the cream is fully incorporated and the mixture is smooth. Stir in the salt.

Leave to cool for 10 minutes in the pan, then pour into a glass bowl and leave until it reaches room temperature.

FOR THE COATING

Melt and temper the milk chocolate, following the method on p.26. Using the detailed instructions on p.29, fill the praline mould with a layer of melted chocolate. Once it's set, pipe in your filling, then seal with a top layer of melted chocolate.

Fresh Mint Leaf Chocolates

An elegant take on the traditional indulgent after-dinner treat. Using fresh mint instead of peppermint gives these chocolates a luxurious feel.

GANACHE FILLING
200g white chocolate, chopped, or callets
180ml double cream
18ml honey
3 fresh mint leaves

COATING
450g dark chocolate, chopped, or callets

Fine mesh strainer
28-hole praline mould

Makes 28 chocolates

FOR THE GANACHE FILLING
Place the white chocolate in a heatproof bowl and set aside.

In a small saucepan, bring the cream and honey to a simmer, then add the mint leaves.

Remove from the heat and allow to steep for 30 minutes, before straining the mixture through a fine mesh strainer into a pan.

Gently reheat the cream until steaming.

Pour the cream over the chocolate and mix together until the chocolate has fully melted and combined with the cream.

Transfer the mixture to a piping bag, cut off the end, then refrigerate until firm.

FOR THE COATING
Melt and temper the chocolate, following the method on p.26. Referring to the detailed instructions on p.29, fill the praline mould with a layer of melted chocolate. Once it's set, pipe in your ganache filling, then seal with a top layer of melted chocolate.

Lemon & Basil Chocolates

This may seem an unusual combination but the savoury notes of basil complement the tartness of lemon. It tastes great encased in either white chocolate or dark. As well as making a delicious filling for use with praline moulds you can also use this recipe to make hand-rolled truffles.

GANACHE FILLING
Zest of 1 lemon
200ml double cream
3 large basil leaves
200g white chocolate,
    chopped, or callets

COATING
450g dark or white choco-
    late, chopped, or callets

Disposable piping bag
28-hole praline mould

Makes 28 chocolates

FOR THE GANACHE FILLING
Grate the lemon zest into a small dish and set aside. In a small pan over a medium heat, heat the cream and basil leaves stirring constantly until bubbles form around the edges of the pan. Let it cool, then leave to rest for about 1 hour. Remove the basil leaves from the cream.

Place the 200g white chocolate in a heatproof bowl. Reheat the cream gently until it begins to bubble. Pour over the chocolate and stir until combined and the chocolate has melted.

Gently stir in the lemon zest. Leave the mixture to cool. When cool, refrigerate until firm and then transfer to a piping bag with the end cut off.

FOR THE COATING
Melt and temper the chocolate, using the method on p.26.

Following the detailed instructions on p.29, fill the praline mould with a layer of melted chocolate. Once it's set, pipe in your ganache filling, then seal with a top layer of melted chocolate.

Rose & Lychee Chocolates

Both floral and fruity, this unusual combination is feminine and delightful.
The flavour was inspired by a perfume launch we recently made cakes for.

GANACHE FILLING
150g fresh lychees
180ml double cream
200g white chocolate,
  chopped, or callets
2 tsp rose extract

COATING
450g dark chocolate,
  chopped, or callets

Disposable piping bag
28-hole praline mould

Makes 28 chocolates

FOR THE GANACHE FILLING
Peel the lychees and remove their stones. Use a blender to purée the lychees or mash them with a fork. Set aside.

Place the white chocolate in a medium-sized heatproof bowl and set aside.

In a small pan over medium heat, heat the cream and lychee purée together, and bring to the boil.

Gently pour the cream over the chocolate and stir until combined and the chocolate has melted. Add the rose extract, then leave the mixture to cool.

Refrigerate until firm, then transfer the mixture to a piping bag and cut the end off.

FOR THE COATING
Melt and temper the chocolate, using the method on p.26.

Following the detailed instructions on p.29, fill the praline mould with a layer of melted chocolate. Once it's set, pipe in your ganache filling, then seal with a top layer of melted chocolate.

Bourbon Whiskey Pralines

This recipe borrows from an anonymous source – my sister brought me a gift from America: bourbon pralines that were so delicious I decided to make my own. I've started putting them in everything, including chocolates.

PRALINE
100g pecans, coarsely
    chopped and toasted
250g golden caster sugar
100ml bourbon

GANACHE FILLING
250g milk chocolate,
    chopped, or callets
200ml double cream

COATING
450g dark chocolate,
    chopped, or callets

Large rolling pin
Disposable piping bag
28-hole praline mould
Baking sheet
Baking paper

Makes 28 pralines

FOR THE PRALINE
Place the toasted pecans on a baking sheet lined with baking paper and set aside.

Combine the sugar with the bourbon in a saucepan over a high heat and cook until the mixture turns into an amber-coloured syrup. Immediately pour the syrup over the pecans and leave to cool.

When cool, break into small pieces then place in a sealable plastic bag and crush with a large rolling pin. Transfer to a food processor and process until the praline is finely ground.

FOR THE GANACHE FILLING
Put the milk chocolate into a medium-sized heatproof bowl. In a pan, bring the cream to a boil and pour straight onto the chocolate. Stir until smooth and combined, let it cool slightly, then stir in the ground praline.

Transfer to a piping bag, snip the end of the bag off and leave the mixture to set in the fridge for 15 minutes before piping into your praline mould.

FOR THE COATING
Melt and temper the dark chocolate, following the method on p.26. Using the detailed instructions on p.29, fill the praline mould with a layer of melted chocolate. Once it's set, pipe in your ganache filling, then seal with a top layer of melted chocolate.

Passion Fruit Chocolates

Passion fruit and white chocolate – an exotic yet classic combination. Passion fruit is not as readily available as some other flavours so these chocolates make a really special gift.

GANACHE FILLING
100g white chocolate, chopped, or callets
3 passion fruit
100ml double cream
½ tbsp honey
10g unsalted butter, at room temperature

COATING
450g white chocolate, chopped, or callets

Sieve
Disposable piping bag
28-hole praline mould

Makes 28 chocolates

FOR THE GANACHE FILLING
Place the 100g chocolate in a heatproof bowl and set aside.

Cut open the passion fruit, remove the pulp and place in a sieve fitted over a small saucepan. Strain the pulp through the sieve, and discard the seeds.

Stir in the cream and honey, then bring the mixture to a soft boil. Pour the cream mixture over the chocolate and stir until chocolate is melted and combined. Stir in the butter.

Transfer the mixture to a piping bag, cut the end off and refrigerate until firm.

FOR THE COATING
Melt and temper the 450g chocolate, using the method on p.26.

Following the detailed instructions on p.29, fill the praline mould with a layer of melted chocolate. Once it's set, pipe in your ganache filling, then seal with a top layer of melted chocolate.

Butterscotch Chews

I just love butterscotch for its traditional feel. It is made with dark brown sugar and has a chewy toffee texture.

BUTTERSCOTCH
75g unsalted butter, plus
    extra for greasing the tin
250g golden caster sugar
125g dark muscovado sugar
1 tsp cider or white wine
    vinegar
125ml glucose syrup
75ml water
¼ tsp salt
½ tsp vanilla extract

COATING
450g dark chocolate,
    chopped, or callets

20cm square cake or
    baking tin
Baking paper
Cook's thermometer
3-prong dipping fork

Makes approx. 64 chews

Line your cake or baking tin with kitchen foil, extending the foil about 5cm above the sides of the tin, then grease the top of the foil. Line a baking sheet with baking paper.

FOR THE BUTTERSCOTCH
Place the sugars, vinegar, syrup, water and salt in a medium saucepan over a medium to high heat. Stir continuously while the sugars dissolve, then insert a thermometer and heat until the temperature reaches 120°C. Follow the instructions on p.178 if you don't have a cook's thermometer.

Stir in the 75g butter and continue to heat, stirring until the temperature reaches 129°C.

Immediately remove the pan from the heat and add the vanilla, mixing until it is well incorporated. Pour the mixture into the prepared cake tin and leave to set at room temperature for several hours or overnight.

Once it's set, pull on the foil to remove the butterscotch from the tin and place face down on a chopping board or clean, flat surface. Peel off the foil and use a sharp knife to cut the butterscotch into 2.5cm squares.

FOR THE COATING
Melt and temper the chocolate, using the method on p.26.

Following the dipping instructions on p.30, dip the butterscotch squares, one at a time, into the chocolate. Place on the lined baking sheet and leave to set, about 5 minutes.

Pistachio Marzipan & Raspberry Diamonds

Marzipan is an underrated ingredient and here it is paired with pistachios to give it a modern spin. The layer of fresh raspberry jelly adds a welcome tartness to offset the sweet nuttiness.

PISTACHIO MARZIPAN
50g pistachios, toasted
1½ tsp flavourless nut oil
225g marzipan

RASPBERRY PASTE
250g fresh raspberries
10g pectin (in powder form)
250g golden caster sugar

COATING
450g dark chocolate,
  chopped, or callets
Freeze-dried raspberry
  powder, to decorate
  (optional)

22cm square cake or baking
  tin
Cling film
Rolling pin
Cook's thermometer
3-prong dipping fork

Makes approx. 25 diamonds

Line your cake or baking tin with cling film.

FOR THE PISTACHIO MARZIPAN
In a food processor, grind the pistachios with the oil until a paste forms. Add the pistachio paste to the marzipan and knead together until everything is fully incorporated. Roll out into the prepared tin.

FOR THE RASPBERRY PASTE
Heat the raspberries in a small pan with a little water, then mash them with a fork.

Tip the pectin into a large, heavy-bottomed pan and mix in the sugar a little at a time to prevent clotting.

Add the raspberry pulp, mix together and bring to the boil. Heat until the temperature reaches 108°C. Follow the instructions on p.178 if you don't have a cook's thermometer. Pour the mixture into the tin over the marzipan and leave to set.

When set, turn out the marzipan and fruit paste onto a clean, flat surface and, using a sharp knife, cut 6 rows across the width, then cut diagonally across to form diamond shapes. Keep them so that the fruit paste sits on top of the marzipan for dipping.

FOR THE COATING
Melt and temper the chocolate, using the method on p.26.

Following the dipping instructions on p.30, dip the marzipan pieces, one at a time, into the tempered chocolate. Place on baking paper to set. Decorate with ground pistachios or freeze-dried raspberry powder.

Fig, Honey & Walnut Chocolates

Being of Mediterranean origin, figs are one of my favourite fruits and are only in season for a short time, making them all the more special. Fig and walnut make an ideal pairing and the honey adds a sweetness that takes me back to hot childhood summers at Fig Tree Bay in Cyprus.

FIG PASTE
10g pectin (in powder form)
200g golden caster sugar
50ml honey
250g fresh figs, puréed

WALNUT PASTE
225g hazelnuts, toasted
225g icing sugar
225g milk chocolate, melted

COATING
450g dark chocolate, finely chopped, or callets

20cm square baking tin
Cling film
Cook's thermometer (optional)
3-prong dipping fork
Baking paper

Makes 64 squares

Line the baking tin with cling film.

FOR THE FIG PASTE
Tip the pectin into a large heavy-bottomed pan and mix in the sugar a little at a time to prevent the pectin from clotting.

Add the honey and the fig purée, mix together and bring to the boil. Heat until the temperature reaches 108°C. Follow the instructions on p.178 if you don't have a cook's thermometer.

Pour the mixture into the prepared tin and leave to set.

FOR THE WALNUT PASTE
Grind the toasted nuts and a quarter of the sugar in a food processor until oily. Add the remaining sugar and the melted milk chocolate and mix into a smooth paste. Pour into the tin over the top of the fig paste.

Refrigerate until firm, then remove from the tin and cut into 64 squares.

TO COAT
Melt and temper the dark chocolate, using the method on p.26. Following the detailed instructions on p.30, dip each square into the chocolate, one at a time, and place on a sheet of baking paper to set.

Caramel & Hazelnut Squares

Imagine a home-made version of Nutella, layered over chewy caramel and enrobed in milk chocolate. Sounds like a dream, which is exactly what this recipe is.

CARAMEL
40g unsalted butter, diced, plus extra for greasing the tin
150ml double cream
250g golden caster sugar
65ml golden syrup
30ml honey
½ tsp vanilla extract

HAZELNUT CREAM
110g dark chocolate, chopped, or callets
110g hazelnuts, toasted
110g icing sugar

22cm square cake or baking tin
Baking paper
Cook's thermometer
3-prong dipping fork

Makes approx. 64 squares

Grease the cake tin and line with baking paper, letting the paper extend about 5cm above the sides of the tin. Line a baking sheet with baking paper.

FOR THE CARAMEL
Pour the cream into a heavy-bottomed pan and bring to a boil over a medium to high heat. Add the sugar, syrup and honey and bring back to the boil.

Using a thermometer, allow the temperature to reach 125°C before removing the pan from the heat. Follow the instructions on p.178 if you don't have a cook's thermometer.

Add the 40g butter and the vanilla, stirring until the butter melts.

Pour the mixture into the prepared cake tin and leave to set. When it's ready, the caramel should have thickened and be firm to the touch.

FOR THE HAZELNUT CREAM
Melt the chocolate in a bain-marie.

Grind the nuts and a quarter of the icing sugar in a food processor until oily.

Add the remaining sugar and the chocolate and mix into a smooth paste. Spread over the top of the firmed caramel and chill until set.

(*continues overleaf*)

Once set, remove the caramel and hazelnut cream layers from the tin and place face down on a chopping board or clean, flat surface. Peel off the baking paper and use a sharp knife to cut the layers into 2.5cm squares.

FOR THE COATING
Melt and temper the chocolate, using the method on p.26.

Follow the dipping instructions on p.30 and dip the squares, one at a time, into the tempered chocolate. Place on the lined baking sheet and leave to set, about 5 minutes.

Crème Brûlée Chocolates

Crème brûlée – a dessert that captures many hearts, including my own. There's nothing I like better than smashing through that layer of caramelised sugar to get to the divine creamy custard underneath. Here's a quirky twist on the classic recipe, inside a chocolate cup. It even has its own caramelised sugar decoration.

CRÈME BRÛLÉE
200ml double cream
1 vanilla pod
25g golden caster sugar
2 large egg yolks

CARAMELISED SUGAR DECORATION
150g granulated sugar
50ml water

CHOCOLATE COATING
450g milk chocolate, chopped, or callets

Fine mesh strainer
4 small ramekins
Deep baking tin
Rolling pin
28-hole chocolate cup mould
Cling film

Makes 28 chocolates

Preheat the oven to 150°C/130°C fan/gas 2.

FOR THE CRÈME BRÛLÉE
Scrape the seeds from the vanilla pod. Combine half the double cream with the vanilla seeds and sugar in a saucepan and bring to a boil over a medium heat. Stir occasionally to prevent a skin from forming.

Once boiled, remove from the heat and let it steep for 15 minutes, then stir in the remaining cream to cool down the mixture.

Whisk the egg yolks together in a large bowl until blended together. Continue whisking as you slowly pour the beaten eggs into the cream mixture. Make sure the cream has cooled enough so that the eggs won't curdle.

Push the mixture through a fine mesh strainer into a jug, then pour into your ramekins.

Place the filled ramekins into a deep baking tin, then pour enough boiling water into the tin to come halfway up the sides of the ramekins, taking care not to splash water into the custard.

Bake for about 30 minutes or until the custard gives a gentle wiggle when moved.

Transfer the baked ramekins to a cooling rack. Leave to cool for 2 hours, then cover the ramekins with cling film and set aside.

(*continues overleaf*)

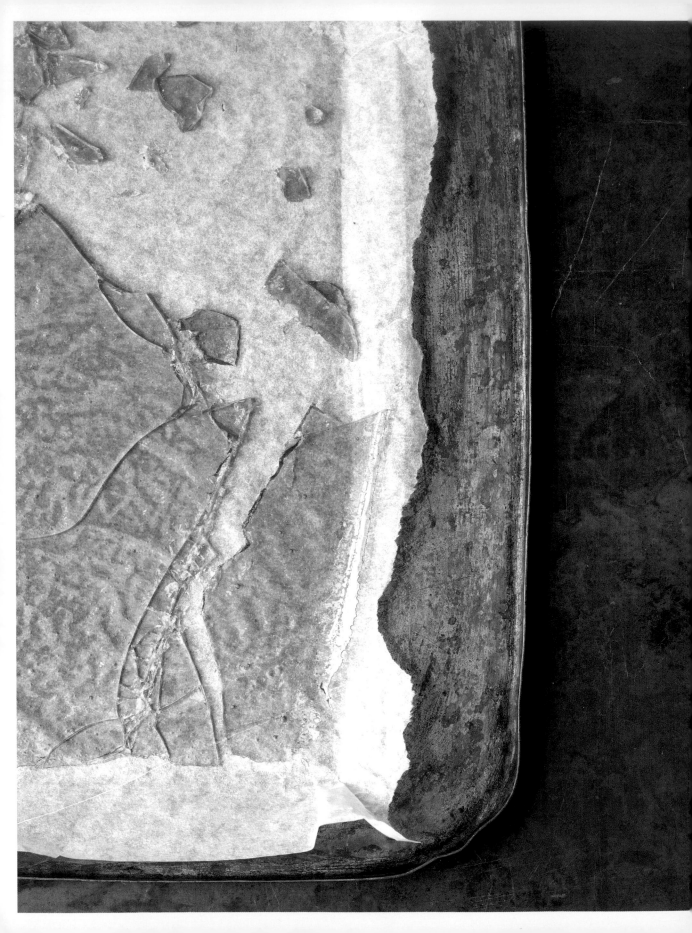

FOR THE CARAMELISED SUGAR DECORATION

Place a sheet of baking paper on a baking tray.

In a large saucepan, combine the sugar and water. Heat on a medium heat until the sugar has dissolved and turned an amber colour, then pour onto the prepared tray.

Once it's cooled completely and set (about 30 minutes), use a rolling pin to crush the sugar into shards of caramel, and set aside.

FOR THE COATING

Melt and temper the chocolate, following the instructions on p.26. Fill the chocolate cup moulds with the tempered chocolate, using the method on p.29 but without sealing off the moulds. Once the chocolate is set, turn the cups out onto a clean work surface.

TO FINISH

Using a spoon, scoop out the crème brûlée from the ramekins and place in a bowl. Gently stir to smooth out any lumps, then pour into a piping bag. Cut off the end of the piping bag and fill the moulds with the custard.

To decorate, press a shard of caramelised sugar into each cup and leave custard to set.

Matcha & Pistachio White Chocolate Truffles

Matcha is essentially a powdered green tea that is widely used in the Far East both as a drink and as an ingredient in baking and sweets. I've added pistachios to this recipe too, for an East-meets-West truffle fusion.

GANACHE FILLING
200g white chocolate, chopped, or callets
½ tsp matcha powder, sifted
200ml double cream
2 tbsp pistachios, finely chopped and toasted

COATING
450g white chocolate, chopped, or callets
100g pistachios, toasted and finely ground

Disposable piping bag (optional)
Vinyl gloves (optional)

Makes approx. 40 truffles

FOR THE GANACHE FILLING
Place the chocolate in a medium-sized heatproof bowl and set aside.

Pour the sifted matcha powder into a small heatproof bowl.

Heat the cream in a small saucepan over a medium heat. Bring to the boil then pour over the matcha powder, and stir until smooth and combined. Immediately pour this mixture over the chocolate. Stir gently until the mixture is smooth and all the chocolate has melted and combined with the cream. Transfer to a piping bag with the end cut off, then chill until firm.

FOR THE COATING
Melt and temper the white chocolate, following the instructions on p.26. Either hand-roll the truffles, using the method on p.32, or use as a filling for moulded chocolates by following the instructions on p.29. In the meantime place the ground pistachios in a small bowl.

Roll the truffles in the ground pistachios and keep chilled until ready to serve. You can also roll the truffles in matcha powder.

Cinnamon Log Truffles

The woody notes of cinnamon instantly add a mild spice to a ganache.
Try pairing with orange zest to give these sinfully rich truffles a festive twist.

GANACHE FILLING
200g dark chocolate,
   chopped, or callets
180ml double cream
1 tsp ground cinnamon

COATING
50g cinnamon
50g icing sugar
450g milk chocolate,
   chopped, or callets

Disposable piping bag
Vinyl gloves (optional)
Cling film
Baking paper

Makes approx. 40 truffles

FOR THE GANACHE FILLING
Place the dark chocolate in a medium-sized heatproof bowl and set aside.

Heat the cream in a small saucepan over a medium heat. Bring to the boil and immediately pour over the chocolate. Stir gently until the mixture is smooth and all the chocolate has melted and combined with the cream. Mix in the cinnamon. Cover the bowl with cling film and chill until firm.

When firm, transfer the ganache into a piping bag and cut off the end. On a sheet of baking paper, pipe the ganache into a long log shape and cut into 5cm-thick portions.

FOR THE COATING
Sift the cinnamon and icing sugar together in a small bowl and set aside.

Melt and temper the chocolate, following the instructions on p.26.

Either hand-roll the truffles, using the method on p.32, or use as a filling for moulded chocolates by following the instructions on p.29.

Immediately roll the truffles in the cinnamon and icing sugar mixture, then place on baking paper to set. Store at room temperature until ready to serve.

Espresso Truffles

A grown-up truffle for coffee lovers. This delightful combination, which uses milk chocolate, adds a contrasting sweetness to the bitter espresso, but you can use dark chocolate if you prefer.

GANACHE FILLING
200g milk chocolate, chopped, or callets
180ml double cream
1 tsp instant espresso powder
1 tsp coffee liqueur (optional)

COATING
450g milk chocolate, chopped, or callets

Disposable piping bag
Vinyl gloves (optional)

Makes approx. 40 truffles

FOR THE GANACHE FILLING
Place the 200g milk chocolate in a medium-sized heatproof bowl and set aside.

Heat the cream and espresso powder together in a small saucepan over a medium heat until the mixture bubbles around the edges, about 3 minutes. Stir until smooth and combined.

Immediately pour this mixture over the chocolate. Stir gently until the mixture is smooth and all the chocolate has melted and combined with the cream. Stir in the liqueur, if using.

Transfer to a piping bag and cut the end off, then chill until firm.

Line a baking sheet with baking paper. Pipe small balls of ganache onto the lined baking sheet, then place in the fridge to set.

Once set, take one ball at a time and, wearing vinyl gloves, roll it in your hands to create a smooth round truffle. Put it back onto the sheet and then into the fridge to set.

FOR THE COATING
Melt and temper the chocolate, using the method on p.26. Either hand-roll the truffles, using the method on p.32, or use as a filling for moulded chocolates by following the instructions on p.29.

Strawberry Champagne Truffles

Champagne brings an extravagance to these chocolates, which makes them perfect for celebrations. But you can skip the champagne if you prefer because the strawberry filling tastes exquisite on its own too.

GANACHE FILLING
200g white chocolate, chopped, or callets
3 large strawberries, hulled
200ml double cream
2 tsp Champagne (optional)

COATING
450g white chocolate, chopped, or callets

DECORATION
Freeze-dried strawberry powder (optional)

Fine mesh strainer
Disposable piping bag
Vinyl gloves (optional)

Makes approx. 30–40 truffles

FOR THE GANACHE
Place the chocolate in a medium-sized heatproof bowl and set aside.

Heat the strawberries with a small amount of water in a saucepan to soften them. Use a fork to mash them, then set aside.

Pour the cream into a small saucepan and bring to the boil. Strain the strawberry purée into the cream through a fine mesh strainer to remove the seeds.

Pour the strawberry cream over the chocolate and stir until the chocolate is fully melted and combined. Add the Champagne, if using, and stir in. You should end up with a thick and glossy mixture.

Pour the mixture into a disposable piping bag with the end cut off and place in the freezer for 1 hour. Strawberry ganache can be very runny so it's best to freeze it both before and after rolling into balls.

FOR THE COATING
Melt and temper the chocolate, following the method on p.26.

Referring to the instructions on p.32, put on vinyl gloves and hand-roll the truffles in the tempered chocolate. Alternatively, use the ganache as a filling for moulded chocolates, following the instructions on p.29.

OPTIONAL
You can decorate these truffles with freeze-dried strawberry powder and it's best to roll the truffles in the powder before the chocolate sets.

Orange & Lavender Truffles

Citrus meets floral. These are two flavours that pack a punch but work harmoniously together. If you favour one over the other you can make your own combinations.

GANACHE FILLING
200ml double cream
2 tsp culinary lavender buds
200g dark chocolate,
    chopped, or callets
Zest of ½ orange

COATING
450g dark chocolate,
    chopped, or callets
100g cocoa powder, to
    decorate (optional)

Disposable piping bag
Vinyl gloves (optional)
Baking sheet
Baking paper

Makes approx. 40 truffles

Line a baking sheet with baking paper.

FOR THE GANACHE FILLING
In a small pan over a medium heat, warm the cream and lavender buds until bubbles form around the edges of the pan. Leave to cool and rest for about 1 hour.

Strain the cream into a pan to remove the lavender buds.

Place the 200g chocolate in a heatproof bowl. Reheat the cream gently and pour over the chocolate. Stir until the chocolate has melted and combined with the cream. Gently stir in the orange zest and leave the mixture to cool.

Refrigerate until firm, then transfer the mixture to a piping bag, cut off the end and pipe walnut-sized blobs onto the lined baking sheet.

FOR THE COATING
Melt and temper the 450g chocolate, using the method on p.26.

Put on vinyl gloves and hand-roll the truffles into balls, following the detailed instructions on p.32, then immediately roll in the cocoa powder (if using). Alternatively, use the ganache as a filling for moulded chocolates, following the instructions on p.29.

Candied Citrus Sticks

Delicious and festive – but who says these treats are just for Christmas?
Swap the oranges in the recipe for any citrus fruit, using the guide below.
Try candied lemon with white chocolate or lime with dark chocolate.

CANDIED PEEL
4 oranges
450g golden caster sugar
1 litre water

COATING
150g golden caster sugar
200g dark chocolate,
    chopped, or callets

Baking sheet
Baking paper

Makes approx. 30–40 citrus
    sticks and slices

**SUBSTITUTING
DIFFERENT CITRUS
FRUITS**
As a general guide when
substituting different citrus
fruit in this recipe, count
1 small lemon or lime as
half an orange, and half a
grapefuit as 1 whole orange.

FOR THE CANDIED PEEL
Wash and dry the fruit. Cut each of the fruit in half. Use a sharp knife to score the rind of 4 halves into quarters. Peel carefully, then cut away the pith. Slice the peel into long, thin strips about 1cm thick. Set aside. Cut the other 4 halves into thin slices.

Combine the sugar and water in a medium-sized saucepan over a medium heat. Stir to dissolve the sugar and heat for 8–10 minutes until the sugar boils. Add the prepared fruit, then turn the heat down to low, until just simmering. Cook at a simmer for about 1 hour, or until the syrup reduces to a quarter of its original volume. Do not stir. Instead, swirl the pan to ensure all of the fruit gets evenly covered.

Remove from the heat and allow to cool. Drain the fruit in a colander.

FOR THE COATING
Preheat the oven to 110°C/90°C fan/gas ¼ and line a baking sheet with baking paper.

Place the sugar in a small bowl. Roll each piece of fruit in the sugar until completely coated and place on the lined baking sheet. Add more sugar if necessary.

Place in the oven for 1 hour to dry out. Check every 20 minutes to make sure they are not burning.Once the pieces are completely dry, leave to cool then scrape off any excess sugar.

Melt and temper the chocolate, following the instructions on p.26. By hand, dip half of each piece of fruit into the melted chocolate, and place on a sheet of baking paper to set.

Caramel Pecan Clusters

Dark caramel shards and toasted pecans, coated in dark chocolate, make for a quick and easy but luxurious treat.

CARAMEL
250g golden caster sugar

CLUSTERS
450g dark chocolate, chopped, or callets
200g pecans, coarsely chopped and toasted

Cook's thermometer (optional)
Rolling pin
Baking sheet
Baking paper

Makes approx. 12 clusters

FOR THE CARAMEL

Line a baking sheet with baking paper. Pour the sugar in an even layer into a large heavy-bottomed pan and place over a medium heat. After about 5 minutes, the sugar should start to melt and liquefy at the edges first.

Once the sugar starts to brown at the edges, do not stir. Instead, simply swirl the pan to prevent it burning. Burnt caramel can't be saved so don't let it get too dark at this stage – it should start to go a mellow brown colour.

Lower the heat right down and stir as little as possible until it turns a rich copper colour. If you have a thermometer, the reading should reach 140°C. Follow the instructions on p.178 if you don't have a cook's thermometer. Carefully pour the caramel onto the lined baking sheet and leave to cool.

Once it has cooled and set, break the caramel up into shards. Place the shards in a sealable plastic bag and use a rolling pin to crush them into small pieces.

FOR THE CLUSTERS

Line a baking sheet with baking paper.

Melt and temper the chocolate, following the method on p.26.

In a bowl combine the caramel pieces and pecans. Stir in the tempered chocolate.

Drop about 12 tablespoonfuls of the mixture onto the lined baking sheet and leave to set.

Toffee Popcorn Peanut Clusters

Salt meets sweet again in a fun and delicious recipe for a simple treat. This is a great recipe for a kids' party.

POPCORN
1 tbsp sunflower oil
40g popcorn kernels

TOFFEE
30g unsalted butter
60g dark muscovado sugar
80ml golden syrup
50ml double cream

CLUSTERS
450g milk chocolate, chopped, or callets
200g roasted salted peanuts, coarsely chopped

Makes approx. 12 clusters

FOR THE POPCORN
Heat the oil in a large, heavy-bottomed saucepan, then sprinkle in the popcorn kernels and coat them evenly in the oil. Cover the pan with a tight-fitting lid, and turn the heat to low.

Listen out for popping sounds, and once the popping quietens down, remove from the heat.

FOR THE TOFFEE
Place the butter, sugar and syrup in a separate heavy-bottomed pan, and slowly bring to the boil. Let the mixture bubble for a few minutes, then carefully add the cream. Cook for a further 2– 3 minutes, then leave to cool until the sauce is thick, sticky and glossy.

Pour the toffee over the popcorn, place the lid back on the pan and shake to mix in the sauce. Leave to cool.

FOR THE CLUSTERS
Line a baking sheet with baking paper.

Melt and temper the chocolate, following the method on p.26.

In a bowl, combine the whole popcorn pieces and the peanuts. Stir in the 450g chocolate.

Drop about 12 tablespoonfuls of the mixture onto the lined baking sheet and leave to set.

MADE IN ENGLAND BY
A. WILKIN LTD.,
 EWCASTLE UPON TYNE

White Chocolate Nut Clusters with Candied Lemon

These clusters look so elegant piled up on a plate. The candied lemon adds zing to the white chocolate while the nuts give it a moreishly crunchy texture.

450g white chocolate, chopped, or callets

100g candied lemon, chopped

100g flaked almonds, lightly toasted

100g pistachios, coarsely chopped and toasted

Baking sheet
Baking paper

Makes approx. 12 clusters

Line a baking sheet with baking paper.

Melt and temper the chocolate, following the method on p.26.

In a bowl, combine the candied lemon pieces, toasted almonds and pistachios. Stir in the tempered chocolate.

Drop about 12 tablespoonfuls of the mixture onto the lined baking sheet and leave to set.

Chocolate-Coated Nuts

Shop-bought chocolate-coated nuts often fall short of the mark. Use a good quality chocolate and make your own to enjoy on the go. This recipe works best with almonds, Brazil nuts or macadamias. Toasting the nuts adds flavour and depth.

100g nuts (unblanched almonds, Brazil nuts or blanched macadamias)
200g golden caster sugar
70ml water
250g dark chocolate, chopped, or callets
65g icing sugar (optional)
65g cocoa powder (optional)

Baking sheet
Baking paper
3-prong dipping fork

Makes approx. 300g

Preheat the oven to 170°C/150°C fan/gas 3.

Spread the nuts evenly on a baking sheet and roast for 5 minutes. Remove from the oven, stir, then return to the oven for 3 more minutes. The nuts should have turned a few shades darker and start to crack and smell nutty. Stir again and return to the oven if needed. This process will take between 8 and 12 minutes. Take care with smaller nuts as they burn more easily.

Remove from the oven and transfer the nuts to a plate or another baking sheet to cool.

Line 2 baking sheets with baking paper.

In a medium saucepan, combine the toasted nuts and the caster sugar with 70ml water. Stir continuously, until the sugar darkens and the nuts are coated completely. Pour the nuts onto the prepared baking sheets and chill immediately for 30 minutes.

Meanwhile, melt the chocolate. Remove the nuts from the fridge and separate any that are stuck together. Transfer half of the nuts into a medium-sized bowl and pour half the tempered chocolate over them. Stir to coat them evenly and then, using a fork, remove them from the chocolate, one by one, and place on one of the lined baking sheets a few centimetres apart. Leave to cool.Repeat with the remaining nuts and chocolate.

Place the icing sugar and cocoa powder (if using) into separate bowls. Toss half of the nuts in the sugar, and the other half in the cocoa, tapping off any excess powder as you go. Leave to set. These will keep in an airtight container for up to 1 month.

BARS AND SLABS

Home-made Caramel Nougat Bars

Give one of the world's most famous chocolate bars a luxury makeover with this delicious recipe that everyone will love.

CHOCOLATE LAYERS (BOTTOM AND TOP)
400g dark chocolate, chopped, or callets

NOUGAT LAYER
225g unsalted butter
200g golden caster sugar
125ml evaporated milk
300ml marshmallow fluff (shop-bought, or see recipe on p.179)
150g smooth peanut butter
1 tsp vanilla extract
200g salted roasted peanuts, roughly chopped

CARAMEL LAYER
300ml double cream
500g golden caster sugar
125ml golden syrup
60ml honey
1 tsp vanilla extract
85g unsalted butter, diced

Butter, for greasing the tin

25cm square cake or baking tin
Baking paper
Cook's thermometer (optional)

Makes approx. 12 bars

Grease and line the cake tin with baking paper, letting the paper extend about 5cm above the sides of the tin.

FOR THE BOTTOM CHOCOLATE LAYER
Melt and temper 200g of the chocolate, following the method on p.26. Pour the tempered chocolate into the prepared baking tin, spreading it evenly. Leave to set.

FOR THE NOUGAT LAYER
Melt the butter in a small saucepan over a medium heat. Add the sugar and evaporated milk, stirring until dissolved. Bring to the boil, then cook for 5 more minutes, stirring occasionally. Add the marshmallow fluff, peanut butter and vanilla and stir until smooth. Turn off the heat and fold in the peanuts. Pour the mixture over the chocolate in the tin and cool completely.

FOR THE CARAMEL LAYER
Pour the cream into a heavy-bottomed pan and bring to the boil over a medium to high heat. Add the sugar, syrup and honey. Bring to the boil again and when the sugar has dissolved or a thermometer dipped into the mixture reaches 125°C, remove from the heat. Follow the instructions on p.178 if you don't have a cook's thermometer. Add the vanilla and butter, stirring until it melts. Pour over the nougat layer and leave to cool and set.

FOR THE TOP CHOCOLATE LAYER
Melt and temper the remaining 200g chocolate (see p.26), then pour it over the caramel. Leave to set.

TO SERVE
Remove from the tin by pulling up the sides of the baking paper, and cut into individual bars with a sharp knife.

Millionaire's Shortbread

This ever-popular treat is made with the richest of ingredients, which is fitting for its name. Shortbread makes for a luxurious biscuit base, with a layer of thick, decadent caramel and the snap of dark chocolate.

SHORTBREAD
150g unsalted butter, softened, plus extra for greasing
80g golden caster sugar
225g plain flour

CARAMEL LAYER
300ml double cream
500g golden caster sugar
125ml golden syrup
60ml honey
1 tsp vanilla extract
85g unsalted butter, diced

CHOCOLATE LAYER
350g dark chocolate, chopped, or callets

20cm square baking tin
Cook's thermometer (optional)
Greaseproof paper

Makes approx. 12 squares

Preheat the oven to 170°C/150°C fan/gas 3. Grease and line the baking tin with greaseproof paper.

FOR THE SHORTBREAD
Using your fingertips, combine the ingredients for the shortbread in a medium-sized bowl to form a smooth dough. Press the dough into the bottom of the prepared tin and prick it with a fork.

Bake for 15–20 minutes or until golden brown. Leave to cool completely.

FOR THE CARAMEL LAYER
Pour the cream into a heavy-bottomed pan and bring to the boil over a medium-high heat. Add the sugar, golden syrup and honey. Bring to the boil again and when the sugar has dissolved or a thermometer dipped into the mixture reaches 125°C, remove from the heat. Follow the instructions on p.178 if you don't have a cook's thermometer. Add the vanilla and butter, stirring until the butter melts. Pour over the shortbread and leave to cool and set.

FOR THE CHOCOLATE LAYER
Melt and temper the chocolate, using the method on p.26, then pour it over the cooled caramel. Leave to set then cut into 12 squares.

Toffee Crisp

This is a personal childhood favourite. It's for those with a sweet tooth – children will love it.

TOFFEE
65g dark muscovado sugar
75ml golden syrup
30g unsalted butter
60ml double cream
50g puffed rice cereal
   (e.g. Rice Krispies)
100g marshmallow fluff
   (shop-bought, or see
   recipe on p.179)

COATING
200g milk chocolate,
   chopped, or callets

22cm square cake or
   baking tin
Baking paper

Makes 12 bars

Line the cake tin with baking paper, letting the paper extend about 5cm above the sides of the tin.

FOR THE TOFFEE
Place the sugar, syrup and butter in a pan and bring slowly to the boil. Let the mixture bubble for a few minutes, then carefully add the cream. Cook for a further 2 or 3 minutes, then leave to cool until the sauce is thick, sticky and glossy.

Place one third of the toffee into a small bowl and set aside to cool.

Add the marshmallow fluff to the larger portion of toffee and stir until combined. Mix together with the rice cereal, then pour into the cake tin and spread until evenly coated. Refrigerate to set.

Once cooled, pour the remaining third of toffee over the rice cereal and leave to set.

FOR THE COATING
Melt and temper the milk chocolate, following the instructions on p.26. Pour the tempered chocolate over the toffee layer and smooth over until it fills the tin. Leave to set.

TO SERVE
When ready to serve, remove from the tin by pulling up the sides of the baking paper, and cut into individual bars with a sharp knife.

Crunchy Honeycomb

Golden caster sugar gives a rich taste to these golden nugget-like treats. It's always fun to watch the mixture foam up when you put the bicarbonate of soda into the sugar and syrup mixture. It's an awesome process, and making this honeycomb is almost as enjoyable as eating it.

HONEYCOMB
72ml golden syrup
200g golden caster sugar
1 tbsp water
3 tsp bicarbonate of soda

COATING
450g milk or dark chocolate, chopped, or callets

22cm square cake or baking tin
Cling film
Cook's thermometer (optional)
3-prong dipping fork
Baking paper

Makes approx. 30 shards

Line the cake tin with cling film, leaving a 5cm overhang.

FOR THE HONEYCOMB
Heat the golden syrup and sugar together in a large, heavy-bottomed saucepan until the sugar has melted or the temperature reaches 140°C. Follow the instructions on p.178 if you don't have a cook's thermometer. Bring to the boil, then simmer on a low heat for 5–10 minutes.

Remove the pan from the heat and carefully add the bicarbonate of soda. Mix this in, working quickly, as it will begin to foam up upon contact. Immediately pour into the cake tin and leave to set.

When set, remove from the tin by pulling on the cling film. Peel off the cling film and cut the honeycomb into shards with a sharp knife.

FOR THE COATING
Melt and temper the chocolate, using the method on p.26.

Following the dipping instructions on p.30, coat the honeycomb shards, one at a time, in the tempered chocolate. Place on a sheet of baking paper and leave to set before serving.

Caramel Dimes

I've always had a soft spot for a certain chocolate bar of the same name but, being a lover of good quality chocolate, have long wished there was a more luxurious version. This is it.

ALMOND CARAMEL SLAB
185g golden caster sugar
60ml golden syrup
100g unsalted butter
135g ground almonds

COATING
450g dark chocolate,
  chopped, or callets

22cm square cake or
  baking tin
3-prong dipping fork
Cling film
Baking paper

Makes approx. 12 bars

Line your cake tin with cling film, leaving a 5cm overhang.

FOR THE ALMOND CARAMEL SLAB
Melt the sugar in a large, heavy-bottomed pan over a medium heat. Do not stir. Once the sugar starts to melt, just swirl the pan to distribute the heat evenly and prevent burning.

Immediately add the syrup and butter. Once the butter has melted add the ground almonds, lower the heat and stir until the mixture no longer sticks to the pan. Pour into the prepared cake tin and spread evenly, using a palette knife, then leave to set.

Once the mixture has cooled and set, pull on the cling film to remove from the tin. Peel off the cling film, then use a sharp knife to cut the caramel into bars about 2.5cm wide.

FOR THE COATING
Melt and temper the chocolate, using the method on p.26.

Following the dipping instructions on p.30, dip the bars, one at a time, in the tempered chocolate. Transfer to a sheet of baking paper and leave to set.

Chocolate Hazelnut Bars

This is a tasty and fun treat to make with kids. Swap the hazelnut butter for peanut butter and the hazelnuts for peanuts for another winning combination.

HAZELNUT CREAM
150g hazelnut butter
80ml golden syrup
80ml honey
65g cocoa powder
75g light muscovado sugar
150ml marshmallow fluff
  (shop-bought, or see
  recipe on p.179)
1 tsp vanilla extract
50g crushed wafer filling
  (see Suppliers on p.180)
  or puffed rice cereal
100g hazelnuts, chopped
  and toasted

CHOCOLATE LAYER
250g milk chocolate,
  chopped, or callets
1 tbsp unsalted butter

Butter or vegetable oil,
  for greasing the tin

25cm square cake or
  baking tin
Baking paper

Makes 12 bars

Grease and line your cake tin with baking paper.

FOR THE HAZELNUT CREAM
Place the hazelnut butter, golden syrup, honey, cocoa powder and muscovado sugar in a large saucepan over a medium heat and bring to the boil. Reduce the heat to low and stir constantly until the mixture is melted and smooth.

Remove from the heat and add the marshmallow fluff. Stir until fully combined. Stir in the vanilla extract, wafer filling and hazelnuts. Pour the mixture into the prepared tin and leave to set.

FOR THE CHOCOLATE LAYER
Melt the milk chocolate in a bain-marie (or in a heatproof bowl set over a pan of simmering water). Add the butter and stir until fully combined. Pour this over the hazelnut cream mixture and leave to set.

TO SERVE
When set, remove from the tin and cut into small squares with a sharp knife.

Chocolate Toffee Slab

This is a show-stopping treat. Break it up into large shards and enjoy all the different textures. It's great for sharing with friends over coffee.

TOFFEE
65g dark muscovado sugar
75ml golden syrup
30g unsalted butter
60ml double cream

SLAB
900g milk chocolate, chopped, or callets
75g whole pecans, toasted
75g whole pistachios, toasted
75g whole macadamias, toasted

1 shallow baking tin measuring 32 x 22cm
Cling film

Makes 1 large slab approx. 32 x 22cm

Line the base and sides of the baking tin with cling film.

FOR THE TOFFEE
Place the sugar, syrup and butter in a pan and bring slowly to the boil. Let the mixture bubble for a few minutes, then carefully add the cream.

Cook for another 2–3 minutes, or until the sauce is thick, sticky and glossy.

Pour into a small heatproof bowl and leave to cool, then place in the fridge.

FOR THE SLAB
Melt and temper the milk chocolate, following the method on p.26.

Spread half of the toasted pecans, pistachios and macadamia nuts in an even layer in the baking tin and pour the chocolate over them. Then immediately scatter the remaining nuts over the chocolate before it sets. Leave the chocolate to cool and set a little.

Once the chocolate has cooled, but not completely set, drizzle the toffee over the chocolate – do not pour the toffee over while the chocolate is still warm or the sudden change in temperature may cause the chocolate to bloom. Leave to set.

TO SERVE
When ready to serve, remove the chocolate toffee slab from the tin, peel off the cling film and break into shards.

Coconut Bars

A delicious coconut ganache is the basis for this decadent take on the Bounty bar. You can use milk or dark chocolate.

COCONUT GANACHE
300g dessicated coconut
200ml double cream
100ml coconut milk
50ml honey
300g white chocolate

COATING
450g dark chocolate, chopped, or callets

22cm square cake or baking tin
3-prong dipping fork
Cling film
Baking paper

Makes approx. 12 bars

Preheat the oven to 150°C/130°C fan/gas 2. Line your cake tin with cling film, leaving a 5cm overhang.

FOR THE COCONUT GANACHE
Spread the dessicated coconut on a baking sheet and toast in the oven for 1 minute at a time, removing from the oven at 1-minute intervals and stirring with a wooden spoon to ensure all of the coconut gets evenly coated. It should take no more than 2–3 minutes to toast the coconut evenly.

In a saucepan, boil the cream, coconut milk and honey together.

Place the white chocolate in a heatproof bowl. Pour the cream mixture over the chocolate and stir until fully combined and the chocolate is melted. Mix in the toasted coconut. Leave to set for several hours or overnight.

Remove the coconut ganache from the tin, peel off the cling film and cut the ganache into 12 rectangles.

FOR THE COATING
Melt and temper the chocolate, using the method on p.26.

Following the dipping instructions on p.30, coat the bars, one at a time, in the tempered chocolate. Place on a sheet of baking paper and leave to set before serving.

Chocolate Flapjacks

A chocolatey take on the traditional flapjack. These are quick and easy to make – ideal if you're in a hurry – and they taste delicious.

400g unsalted butter, plus extra for greasing
200g golden caster sugar
200g light muscovado sugar
100ml golden syrup
600g rolled oats
6 tbsp cocoa powder

25cm square cake or baking tin
Baking paper

Makes 12 flapjacks

Preheat the oven to 180°C/160°C fan/gas 4. Grease and line the cake tin with baking paper.

Place the 400g butter, the sugars and syrup in a large saucepan, and heat gently until the butter has melted. Stir well.

Pour the oats over the butter mixture and stir in, making sure all the oats are evenly coated. Mix in the cocoa powder, then pour the mixture into the prepared tin and spread evenly to ensure the surface is level. Bake for 15–20 minutes or until set. Remove from the oven while still soft as the flapjack will harden as it cools.

Place the tin on a wire cooling rack and, using a sharp knife, cut the flapjack into squares. Leave in the tin until completely cooled.

Raspberry Ripple White Chocolate Slab

Lovers of white chocolate will be delighted with this elegant treat. The fresh raspberry ripple gives the chocolate slab a tart edge and an amazingly vibrant colour.

120g fresh raspberries
2 tbsp golden caster sugar
dash of lemon juice
900g white chocolate,
    chopped, or callets

1 shallow baking tin
    measuring 32 x 22cm
Fine mesh strainer
Cling film

Makes 1 large slab approx.
    32 x 22cm

Line the base and sides of the baking tin with cling film.

Press the raspberries through a mesh strainer set over a bowl to remove the seeds. Stir in the sugar and add a dash of lemon juice to taste.

Melt and temper the chocolate, following the method on p.26.

Pour the tempered chocolate into the prepared tin, spreading it evenly. Leave to cool and set a little. Once the chocolate has cooled, but not completely set, use a spoon to drizzle the raspberry juice over the surface of the chocolate. Then, using a knife or skewer, swirl the raspberry juice through the chocolate to create a rippled effect.

Leave to set before removing from the tin.

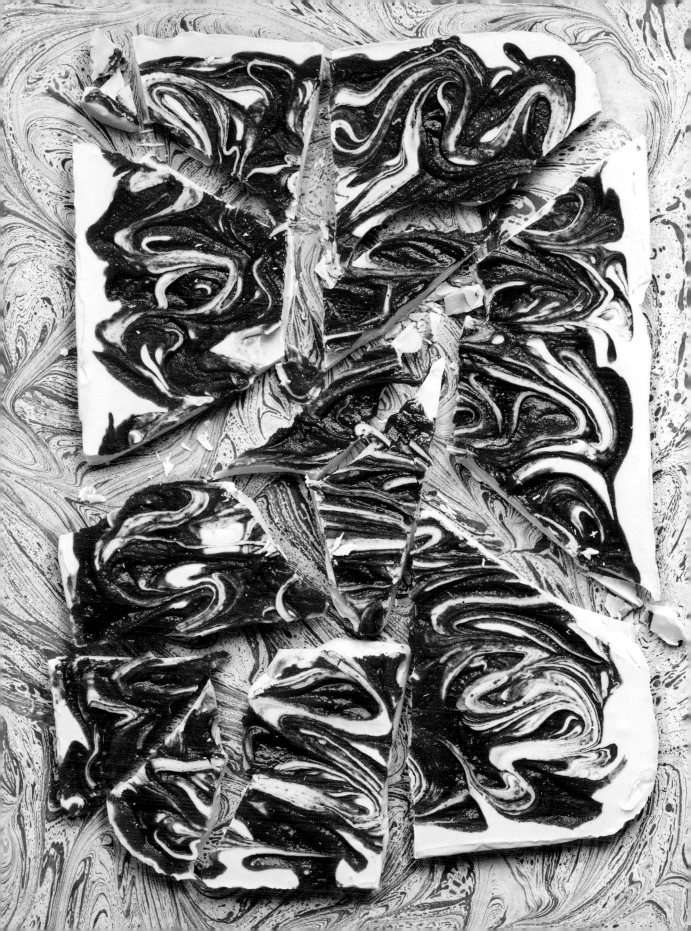

Dark Chocolate Fruit and Nut Slab

Slabs are a very of-the-moment way of shaping chocolate. A slab is simultaneously grand and unfussy. Beautifully wrapped in clear paper and tied with a ribbon, it makes a generous and impressive-looking gift

600g dark chocolate, chopped, or callets
75g sour cherries
75g dried apricots, chopped
75g Brazil nuts, coarsely chopped and toasted
75g whole pistachios, toasted
100g white chocolate

1 shallow baking tin measuring 32 x 22cm
Baking paper

Makes 1 large slab approx. 32 x 22cm

Line the base and sides of the baking tin with baking paper.

Melt and temper the dark chocolate, following the method on p.26.

Spread half of the fruit and nuts over the base of the prepared tin, then pour the tempered dark chocolate over them.

Sprinkle the remaining fruit and nuts over the chocolate and leave to cool.

Melt and temper the white chocolate, following the method on p.26, then drizzle it over the cooled dark chocolate slab.

Leave to set before removing from the tin.

Maple Bacon Chocolate Slab

If you like salt with your sweet, then you might like this surprisingly good treat. The sweet milk chocolate really complements the smoky flavour of crispy bacon made perfectly chewy yet crunchy by the maple syrup.

BACON
400g thick-cut good quality bacon, with fat cut off if you want
72ml maple syrup
1 tsp sea salt (optional)

MAPLE TOFFEE SAUCE
30g unsalted butter
50g light muscovado sugar
pinch of salt
35ml maple syrup

CHOCOLATE SLAB
900g milk chocolate, chopped, or callets

Shallow baking tin measuring 32 x 22cm
Baking paper
Cooking foil

Makes 1 slab approx. 32 x 22cm

Preheat the oven to 200°C/180°C fan/gas 6. Line the base and sides of the baking tin with baking paper.

FOR THE BACON
Cover a baking rack or baking sheet with foil and lay the bacon on it. Bake for 15–20 minutes, or until the bacon begins to brown, turning it over halfway.

Carefully remove the baking rack or sheet from the oven and brush both sides of the bacon with the maple syrup. Return to the oven and bake for another 3–5 minutes, or until the bacon is golden brown.

Transfer the bacon to a plate lined with kitchen paper. Leave to cool completely, then cut into 2.5cm pieces.

FOR THE MAPLE SAUCE
Melt the butter in a saucepan over a medium-high heat. Add the sugar and salt, stirring continuously until the sugar is completely dissolved. Turn down the heat, then boil for 2 more minutes. Add the maple syrup and continue to boil and stir until the sauce is thick and smooth. Remove from the heat and leave to cool but drizzle over slab before it sets.

FOR THE CHOCOLATE SLAB
Melt and temper the chocolate, using the method on p.26.

Place half the bacon in the prepared baking tin, then pour the tempered chocolate over. Arrange the remaining bacon over the top of the chocolate before it sets. Leave to cool slightly and then, using a spoon, drizzle the cooled maple sauce over the top. Leave to set completely, then remove from the tin.

NO BAKES

Chocolate Nougat Fingers

This is a seriously good nougat. In our bakery we love anything containing hazelnuts and pistachios, so this is a firm favourite. In fact, you may find yourself wanting more.

300g golden caster sugar
300ml glucose syrup
1 tsp vanilla bean paste
60ml water
2 large egg whites
40g cocoa powder
100g dark chocolate, chopped, or callets, melted
100g toasted hazelnuts, coarsely chopped and toasted
100g toasted pistachios, coarsely chopped and toasted
Oil, for greasing the tin (optional)

1 baking tin measuring 25 x 15cm
8 sheets rice paper, each measuring 6 x 15cm
Cook's thermometer

Makes approx. 24 fingers

Cover the bottom of the baking tin with 4 of the rice paper sheets. Grease the sides of the tin with a little oil, if you want, as this will help prevent the nougat from sticking.

Place the sugar, syrup, vanilla and water into a large, heavy-bottomed pan, bring it slowly to the boil and keep on the heat until the temperature reaches 121°C, about 15 minutes. Follow the instructions on p.178 if you don't have a cook's thermometer.

Just before the syrup is ready whisk the egg white to stiff peaks with an electric hand whisk or mixer. Remove the syrup from the heat and slowly pour into the egg whites with the mixer going at a medium-high speed. You may want to put a mixer guard on at this point.

The mixture will increase in volume and look shiny like meringue. As soon as all of the syrup has been poured in, add the cocoa powder and melted chocolate. Working quickly, add the nuts.

While this mixture looks like meringue it's much stickier, so you will need to get it all out of the mixer within a minute or so of the syrup being added in.

Pour the mixture into the prepared tin, spreading it evenly over the rice paper with a palette knife or spatula dipped in boiling water. Place the remaining rice paper sheets over the top, pressing them down to stick.

Allow to cool, then place in the fridge for several hours or overnight until set. When set, remove the slab from the baking tin and cut into fingers.

Rocky Road

Chunky, crunchy, gooey, chocolatey. No mouthful is ever the same with this no-bake treat made of marshmallows, chocolate, nuts and biscuit. And if all that is not enough, why not add some sour cherries for the ultimate indulgence?

200g unsalted butter, plus extra for greasing the tin
60ml golden syrup
250g plain chocolate, chopped, or callets, plus extra for drizzling
250g milk chocolate, chopped, or callets
150g digestive biscuits
50g pistachios, chopped and toasted
50g hazelnuts, chopped and toasted
150g mini marshmallows
100g sour cherries (optional)

24cm square cake or baking tin
Baking paper
Rolling pin

Makes approx. 12 bars

Grease and line the cake or baking tin with baking paper.

Melt the 200g butter, the golden syrup and both types of chocolate together in a heavy-bottomed pan over a gentle heat. Scoop out a third of the mixture into a small bowl, and set aside.

Place the digestive biscuits in a plastic bag and crush into small pieces with a rolling pin – you want them to be crumbs but not too fine.

Set aside one third of the nuts and marshmallows. Mix the remaining two thirds of the chopped nuts and marshmallows and all of the crushed biscuits into the melted chocolate mixture plus the sour cherries if wanted. Pour this into the prepared tin and smooth the top with a wet spatula.

Pour the reserved melted chocolate mixture over the top and smooth out. Sprinkle the remaining third of nuts and marshmallows over the top.

Melt a little extra plain chocolate in a bain-marie or in a heatproof bowl set over a pan of simmering water, then drizzle it over the nuts and marshmallows. Chill for at least 2 hours or overnight.

To serve, cut into bars or squares.

Posh Cornflake Treats

Push your nostalgic buttons with these cornflake treats. The dark chocolate gives this recipe a grown-up twist, or you can substitute milk chocolate if making it for children.

70g unsalted butter, plus extra for greasing the tin
200g dark chocolate (50%), chopped, or callets
50ml golden syrup
50g cornflakes
50g puffed rice cereal
Pinch of sea salt (optional)

22cm square cake or baking tin
Baking paper
Round biscuit cutter (optional)

Makes approx. 12 pieces

Grease and line your cake tin with baking paper, extending the paper about 5cm above the tin.

Melt the chocolate in a bain-marie (or in a heatproof bowl set over a pan of simmering water).

Melt the 70g butter in a heavy-bottomed pan over a low heat. Allow to cool slightly, then add the golden syrup and mix together.

Stir in the melted chocolate, then the cornflakes and rice cereal. Add a pinch of sea salt if you want.

Pour the mixture into the prepared tin and, with lightly greased hands, firmly press the mixture down and leave to set. Alternatively, spoon the mixture onto a sheet of baking paper and leave to set.

When set, pull on the baking paper to remove the mixture from the tin, and turn out onto a chopping board or clean, flat surface. Peel off the baking paper and either cut the slab into squares or use a round biscuit cutter to cut into rounds.

White Chocolate Cornflake Cakes

These treats are more gooey than you might imagine and the addition of almonds and shredded coconut gives them texture and crunch. For a playful touch, cut into rounds, almost like little cakes.

70g unsalted butter, plus extra for greasing the tin

200g white chocolate, chopped, or callets, plus extra for drizzling

230ml marshmallow fluff (shop-bought, or see recipe on p.179)

50g cornflakes

50g puffed rice cereal

50g flaked almonds, lightly toasted

50g shredded coconut, lightly toasted

20cm square cake or baking tin

Round biscuit cutter (optional)

Baking paper

Makes approx. 12 pieces

Grease and line your cake or baking tin with baking paper, extending the paper about 5cm above the tin.

Melt the white chocolate in a bain-marie (or in a heatproof bowl set over a pan of simmering water).

Melt the 70g butter in a heavy-bottomed pan over a low heat. Allow to cool slightly, then add the marshmallow fluff and mix together. The marshmallow fluff makes the mixture very sticky, so stir vigorously until it's fully incorporated.

Stir in the melted chocolate and then the cornflakes and rice cereal. Add the toasted almonds and coconut.

Pour the mixture into the prepared tin and, with lightly greased hands, firmly press the mixture down. Leave to set. Melt a little extra chocolate in a bain-marie or heatproof bowl set over a pan of simmering water, and drizzle over the top. Leave to set.

Pull on the baking paper to lift the slab out of the tin, then turn it out onto a chopping board or clean, flat surface. Peel off the paper and cut into squares or use a round biscuit cutter to cut into rounds.

Tiffin

Every spring my husband and I go to Wales and I'm always fascinated by the stalls people set up outside their homes selling home-made treats. You just put money in a pot and pick up a cake or jam or even honey. How I wish we could do that in London! This tiffin recipe was inspired by one particular stall. For years I've promised my husband I'd make him tiffin, but never got around to it. So this recipe is for him.

125g unsalted butter, plus extra for greasing the tin
2 tbsp golden caster sugar
36ml golden syrup
4 tsp cocoa powder
200g shortbread biscuits, crushed
50g sour cherries
250g dark chocolate, chopped, or callets

22cm square cake or baking tin
Baking paper

Makes 20 pieces

Grease and line your cake tin with baking paper.

In a heavy-bottomed saucepan, melt the 125g butter with the sugar, golden syrup and cocoa powder. When melted, stir in the crushed biscuits and the sour cherries.

Pour the mixture into the prepared tin and press down. Leave to chill in the fridge for 1 hour or until set.

Melt and temper the chocolate, following the instructions on p.26. Pour over the mixture in the tin. Leave to set.

To serve, remove the tiffin from the tin and cut into 20 pieces with a sharp knife.

Chocolate & Coffee Double Decker Fudge

Coffee and chocolate – surely a marriage made in heaven. I'm lucky enough to live near some of the best artisan coffee shops in London, so how could I not include an indulgent coffee recipe?

CHOCOLATE FUDGE

60g unsalted butter, plus
    extra for greasing the tin
400g golden caster sugar
170ml glucose syrup
180ml evaporated milk
200g dark chocolate,
    chopped, or callets, melted
½ tsp vanilla bean paste

COFFEE FUDGE

350g golden caster sugar
20ml glucose syrup
150ml evaporated milk
50g unsalted butter
1 tbsp good quality instant
    coffee powder

20cm square cake or
    baking tin
Cook's thermometer
    (optional)
Baking paper

Makes approx. 64 pieces

Grease and line your cake tin with baking paper.

FOR THE CHOCOLATE FUDGE LAYER
Place the sugar, syrup and evaporated milk in a heavy-bottomed saucepan. Bring to a soft boil until the mixture reaches 118°C. Follow the instructions on p.178 if you don't have a cook's thermometer.

Add the 60g butter and return to a soft boil until the temperature reaches 118°C again. Remove from the heat and stir in the chocolate until dissolved.

Mix in the vanilla paste, then pour the fudge into the prepared tin and leave to set for 1 hour.

FOR THE COFFEE FUDGE LAYER
In a heavy-bottomed pan, bring the sugar, syrup and evaporated milk to a soft boil until the mixture reaches 118°C.

Add the butter and return to a soft boil until the temperature reaches 118°C again.

Remove from the heat and stir in the coffee until dissolved.

Pour the mixture over the set chocolate fudge and leave to set for 1 hour.

TO SERVE
Remove from the tin and cut into 64 cubes.

Chocolate Doughnuts

There's something very moreish about a doughnut, especially one filled with gooey, rich chocolate and dusted in cocoa and sugar.

DOUGHNUTS
1 x 7g sachet fast action
   dried yeast
30ml warm water
150ml lukewarm milk
50g golden caster sugar
½ tsp salt
1 large egg
45g unsalted butter,
   plus extra for greasing
470g strong white flour,
   plus extra for dusting
1 litre vegetable oil,
   for frying

CHOCOLATE FILLING
150g dark chocolate,
   chopped, or callets
50ml whipping cream
30ml golden syrup
25g unsalted butter
Pinch of salt

TO DUST
200g golden caster sugar
100g cocoa powder

Cook's thermometer
   (optional)
Piping bag fitted with a
   wide nozzle

Makes 18–20 doughnuts

FOR THE DOUGHNUTS

In a small bowl, sprinkle the yeast over the warm water and leave to stand for 5 minutes or until foamy.

In a large bowl, gently mix the yeast mixture with the milk, 50g caster sugar, salt, egg, 45g butter and 470g flour. Knead for about 5 minutes, or until the dough is smooth and elastic.

Place the dough in a greased bowl and cover with a damp tea towel. Leave to rise in a warm place for 15 minutes until doubled in size. The dough is ready if, when you touch it, an indentation remains.

Turn the dough out onto a floured surface. Break off about 12 ping-pong-ball-sized pieces (about 40g each of dough) and roll into balls. Place on a tray lined with baking paper. Cover with a clean cloth and let the doughnuts sit out to rise until doubled in size.

Heat the oil in a deep fat fryer or heavy-bottomed pan to 190°C (until the oil is bubbling but not smoking). Using a silicone or metal spatula, carefully slide the doughnuts into the oil. Fry the doughnuts two at a time for 30 seconds on each side until golden brown. Carefully remove from the pan and transfer to a wire rack to drain.

(*continues overleaf*)

FOR THE CHOCOLATE FILLING

Melt the chocolate in a bain-marie (or in a heatproof bowl set over a pan of simmering water). Pour in the cream and stir until smooth and combined. Add the golden syrup, butter and salt.

Spoon the filling into a piping bag fitted with a wide nozzle. Use the nozzle to make a hole in the side of each doughnut and pipe a generous amount of filling into the centre.

TO DUST

Combine the caster sugar and cocoa powder in a tray or large bowl and roll each doughnut in the mixture, until completely covered.

Spanish Hot Chocolate

The Spanish are credited with introducing chocolate to the Western world after discovering it in South America some 500 years ago. This is an incredibly rich drink that is a traditional part of a breakfast in Spain. Thick and delicious, it's nothing like the powdered versions.

500ml full-fat milk
1 tsp cornflour
75ml whipping cream
210g dark chocolate, chopped, or callets, plus extra for grating
200g golden caster sugar

Makes approx. 4 servings or 600ml

Combine the milk and cornflour in a medium-sized saucepan. Whisk to dissolve the cornflour, then bring to the boil over a medium heat. Meanwhile, in a clean bowl whisk the cream until it holds stiff peaks, which takes 5–8 minutes.

Remove the milk from the heat and add the chocolate. Stir continuously until the chocolate has melted.

Pour the sugar into the mixture and stir until dissolved. Return the saucepan to a low heat, stirring slowly but continuously for 5–10 minutes. The mixture should thicken quickly. Once thickened, immediately remove from the heat and use a ladle to transfer into cups. Add a dollop of the whipped cream to each, along with a sprinkling of grated chocolate.

Serve piping hot.

Chocolate Marshmallows

While these marshmallows take a while, it's a fun way to spend an afternoon.

9 sheets gelatine leaves
250ml water, plus 200ml
400g golden caster sugar
6ml glucose syrup
2 large egg whites
6 tbsp cocoa powder, plus
  50g for dusting
100g icing sugar, for dusting

20cm square baking tin
Cook's thermometer
  (optional)
Cling film

Makes approx.
  24 marshmallows

Line the base and sides of your baking tin with cling film. In a small bowl soak the gelatine leaves in 250ml water.

Place the sugar, glucose syrup and the 200ml water in a heavy-bottomed saucepan and bring to the boil. Heat until a thermometer reaches 129°C. Follow the instructions on p.178 if you don't have a cook's thermometer. Stir thoroughly and brush down any sugar on the sides of the pan with a wet pastry brush. Add the soaked gelatine to the sugar syrup, then stir the mixture together gently, and pour into a jug.

In a clean, medium-sized mixing bowl, whisk the egg whites until stiff peaks form. Continue to whisk and very slowly pour the sugar syrup into the egg whites. Take care not to let the sugar syrup touch the whisk directly, instead pour it down the side of the bowl – this will stop the marshmallow forming crystals. The mixture should double in volume and become meringue-like. Continue to whisk until the marshmallow becomes very thick and cools a little. When it starts to form stretched bubblegum-like strands, add 6 tablespoons of cocoa powder and whisk until just combined.

Pour into the prepared tin, using a greased spatula to spread it evenly. Leave in a cool dry place to set for 2 hours.

Dust a clean, flat surface with the icing sugar. Remove the marshmallow from the tin and place on the dusted surface. Peel off the cling film and cut into squares, using a greased knife or pizza wheel. Turn each square over on the dusted surface until it is coated on every side.

Chocolate Praline Ice Cream

Pralines are really just nuts set in sugar syrup. This chocolate ice cream tastes good on its own, but even better with a sprinkling of praline. If you're looking for the perfect dinner party dessert, serve this topped with the indulgent chocolate sauce recipe, below.

PRALINE
100g pecans, coarsely
   chopped and toasted
250g golden caster sugar
100ml water

ICE CREAM
120g dark chocolate,
   chopped, or callets
350ml full-fat milk
100g golden caster sugar
4 egg yolks
350ml whipping cream

Rolling pin
Ice-cream maker (optional)
Baking sheet
Baking paper

Serves 12

FOR THE PRALINE
Place the toasted pecans on a baking sheet lined with baking paper, and set aside.

Combine the sugar with the water in a saucepan over a high heat and cook until it forms an amber-coloured syrup. Immediately pour the syrup over the pecans and leave to cool.

When cool, break the coated pecans into small pieces, then place in a sealable plastic bag and crush with a large rolling pin. Transfer to a food processor and process until the praline is roughly ground.

FOR THE ICE CREAM
In a small saucepan, heat the chocolate and milk together gently, stirring until the mixture is smooth and the chocolate has melted. Remove from the heat and set aside to cool slightly.

Place the sugar and egg yolks into a large bowl and whisk until the mixture turns pale and leaves a trail when the whisk is lifted. Slowly add the milk mixture, stirring with a wooden spoon.

Strain the mixture into a medium-sized saucepan and cook over a low heat for 10–15 minutes, stirring continuously. Once the mixture has a custard-like consistency and is thick enough to coat the back of a spoon, remove from the heat. Do not allow the mixture to boil or it will curdle.

Leave the mixture to cool for at least 1 hour, stirring occasionally to prevent a skin forming.

(*continues overleaf*)

In the meantime whip the cream to soft peaks, and keep in the fridge until ready to use.

IF USING AN ICE-CREAM MAKER
Add the whipped cream and fold the custard mixture into the cream. Then churn the mixture according to the manufacturer's instructions. Just before the ice cream freezes, add the praline. Transfer to a freezer container and freeze until required.

IF YOU DON'T HAVE AN ICE-CREAM MAKER
Freeze the custard, uncovered, in a freezer container for 1 hour, or until it begins to set around the edges. Turn the custard out into a bowl and stir with a whisk until smooth, then fold in the whipped cream and praline. Return to the freezer and freeze for a further 2 hours. To store, put a lid on the container and keep in the freezer until ready to serve.

Chocolate Sauce

This indulgent and versatile sauce is great drizzled over all sorts of puddings as well as over ice cream.

300g dark chocolate, chopped, or callets
100ml whipping cream
75ml golden syrup
50g unsalted butter
Pinch of salt

Makes approx. 250ml

Melt the chocolate in a bain-marie (or in a heatproof bowl set over a pan of simmering water), and pour the whipping cream into a jug or bowl.

Pour the melted chocolate over the cream and stir until smooth and combined. Add the golden syrup, butter and salt, and stir until thickened. Serve warm.

You can store this chocolate sauce in the fridge in an airtight container for up to 2 days. Gently reheat to serve.

BAKING WITH CHOCOLATE

Ultimate Chocolate Cake

This cake is divine. I created the recipe especially for this book but the results were so impressive we decided to start using it in the bakery too. The addition of sour cream softens the crumb so the cake melts in your mouth with every bite.

335g unsalted butter, softened, plus extra for greasing the tin
310g self-raising flour
200g cocoa powder
2½ tsp baking powder
¾ tsp bicarbonate of soda
¾ tsp salt
250g golden caster sugar
135g dark muscovado sugar
2 tsp vanilla extract
5 large eggs
335ml sour cream

BUTTERCREAM
500g unsalted butter, softened
1000g icing sugar, sifted
3 tsp vanilla extract
300g dark chocolate (70%), chopped, or callets

GANACHE GLAZE
200g dark chocolate (70%), chopped, or callets
180ml double cream
20g unsalted butter, melted
Edible gold leaf (optional)

3 x 25cm round sandwich cake tins, or 4 x 23cm round sandwich cake tins
Baking paper

Serves 12

Preheat the oven to 180°C/160°C fan/gas 4. Grease and line your cake tins with baking paper.

In a medium-sized bowl, sift together the flour, cocoa powder, baking powder, bicarbonate of soda and salt. Set aside.

In a separate bowl, cream the 335g butter until light and fluffy. Gradually add the sugars and continue creaming for another 5 minutes. Mix in the vanilla extract.

Add the eggs, one at a time, mixing for 1 minute between each addition.

Gently add half the flour mixture and fold in until just combined. Pour in half the sour cream, and then repeat with the remaining flour mixture and sour cream. Fold in after each addition.

Divide the mixture evenly between the cake tins. Bake for 30 minutes, or until a cocktail stick inserted into the centre comes out clean.

Turn out onto a wire rack to cool completely.

FOR THE CHOCOLATE BUTTERCREAM
Melt the chocolate in a bain-marie (or in a heatproof bowl set over a pan of simmering water). Leave to cool. Beat the butter until smooth and creamy, add the sugar gradually and beat until light and fluffy. Beat in the vanilla.

Add the melted chocolate, and beat until fully incorporated.

TO ASSEMBLE THE CAKE

Using a serrated knife, level the tops of the cooled cakes. For a 3-layer cake, put 1 cake onto a cake board or stand, to form the bottom layer, and spread a thick layer of buttercream over it. For the middle layer, place the second cake on top, and repeat the buttercream. Now place the third cake on top and spread a thin layer of buttercream over the top and then the sides of the whole of the layered cake, covering it completely. This is your crumb coat. Place in the fridge to set for 15 minutes. Use the same process for a 4-layer cake.

When set, spread another thick layer of buttercream over the top and sides of the layer cake and use a palette knife to smooth it out.

Place the cake in the fridge for 20 minutes while you make the ganache glaze. This is important if you want the perfect drip effect.

FOR THE GANACHE GLAZE

Place the chocolate in a medium-sized heatproof bowl, and set aside.

Put the cream in a small saucepan over a medium heat. Bring to the boil, then immediately pour over the chocolate.

Stir gently until the mixture is smooth and all the chocolate has melted. Add the softened butter and mix until fully incorporated.

Let the ganache thicken slightly before slowly pouring it over the cake. When pouring, allow the ganache to reach the edges of the cake, then stop pouring. Use a palette knife to push the ganache over the edges, if required, to create fantastic drips.

Decorate with edible gold leaf, if desired.

Black Forest Cupcakes

A little bit kitsch, a little bit boozy, this Black Forest version of the classic chocolate cupcake is a favourite of mine. We decorate them with cocoa nibs and dip the fresh cherries in tempered chocolate.

CUPCAKES
300g griottines (cherries soaked in kirsch)
200g self-raising flour
2 tbsp cocoa powder
1 tsp baking powder
¼ tsp bicarbonate of soda
¼ tsp salt
125g unsalted butter
200g golden caster sugar
2 large eggs
1 tsp vanilla extract
50g chocolate, chopped, or callets, melted

BUTTERCREAM
150g unsalted butter, at room temperature
300g icing sugar, sifted
1 tsp vanilla extract
36ml double cream

TOPPING
Fresh cherries, dipped in melted chocolate
Cocoa nibs or chocolate shavings, to decorate

12-hole muffin tin
12 muffin cases
Sieve
Disposable piping bag

Makes 12

Preheat the oven to 190°C/170°C fan/gas 5. Line a 12-hole muffin tin with muffin cases.

FOR THE CUPCAKES
Using a sieve, drain the cherries with a small bowl underneath to collect the kirsch. Set aside the kirsch and place the cherries in a separate bowl.

In a medium-sized bowl, whisk together the flour, cocoa, baking powder, bicarbonate of soda and salt.

Cream the butter and sugar together until light and fluffy. Add the eggs, one at a time, beating until smooth (about 1 minute each egg). Gently beat in the vanilla.

Add the flour mixture and beat just until incorporated. Do not over-mix. Fold in the melted chocolate and the drained cherries.

Spoon the batter into the muffin cases, filling them about two thirds full. Bake for 16–18 minutes or until a cocktail stick inserted into the centre of a cupcake comes out clean. Place on a wire rack to cool. While the cakes are still slightly warm pour 1 teaspoon of the reserved kirsch over each cupcake.

FOR THE BUTTERCREAM
Beat the butter until smooth and creamy, add the sugar gradually and beat until light and fluffy. Beat in the vanilla and then the cream. Transfer to a piping bag with the end cut off, and pipe onto the cupcakes.

Top the cupcakes with the chocolate-dipped fresh cherries and decorate with cocoa nibs or chocolate shavings.

Dark Brazil Nut Brownies

The dark muscovado sugar makes these brownies extremely rich and gooey, while the toasted Brazil nuts form the perfect complement.

180g unsalted butter, plus
   extra for greasing the tin
180g dark chocolate,
   chopped, or callets
120g plain flour
45g cocoa powder
¼ tsp salt
3 large eggs
100g golden caster sugar
80g dark muscovado sugar
1 tsp vanilla extract
100g Brazil nuts, coarsely
   chopped and toasted

22cm square baking tin
   or brownie tin
Baking apper

Makes 12 squares

Preheat the oven to 180°C/160°C fan/gas 4. Grease and line your baking tin with baking paper.

Melt the 180g butter and chocolate together in a bain-marie (or in a heatproof bowl set over a pan of simmering water).

Sift the flour, cocoa powder and salt together and set aside.

In a separate bowl, mix together the eggs, sugars and vanilla extract until well combined. Stir in the butter and chocolate mixture until thick and creamy.

Mix in the flour and stir until combined.

Fold in the toasted nuts.

Pour into the prepared tin and bake for 15–20 minutes, until the top is cracked and the centre is just set. Leave to cool for 20 minutes, then cut into squares.

Crownies

A crownie is a cookie baked into a brownie. Need I say more?

Makes 12 crownies

BROWNIES
180g unsalted butter, plus
  extra for greasing the tin
120g plain flour, plus extra
  for dusting the tin
180g dark chocolate,
  chopped, or callets
¼ tsp salt
3 large eggs
180g golden caster sugar
1 tsp vanilla extract

COOKIES
140g plain flour
½ tsp salt
¾ tsp baking powder
110g unsalted butter,
  softened
85g golden caster sugar
110g light muscovado sugar
1 tsp vanilla extract
1 egg
50g milk chocolate chips
  or callets

12-hole muffin tin

Makes 12

Grease and flour the muffin tin.

FOR THE BROWNIES
Melt the butter and chocolate together in a bain-marie (or in a heatproof bowl set over a pan of simmering water).

Sift the flour and salt together and set aside.

In a separate bowl, mix together the eggs, sugar and vanilla until well combined. Stir in the butter and chocolate mixture until thick and creamy. Add the flour and stir until combined. Spoon the mixture evenly into the cups in the muffin tin and chill for at least 30 minutes.

FOR THE COOKIES
Sift together the flour, salt and baking powder and set aside.

Cream the butter and sugars together until light and fluffy, then add the vanilla. Add the egg, then slowly mix in the dry ingredients. Stir in the chocolate chips or callets.

Tip the mixture out onto a clean, flat surface and break off tablespoon-sized bits and flatten into patties

Preheat the oven to 180°C/160°C fan/gas 4.
Take the muffin tin out of the fridge and place the cookie patties on top of the brownie mixture. Chill for a further 15 minutes.

When chilled, bake the crownies for 15–18 minutes until the cookie tops are golden brown. Remove from the oven and leave to cool completely before turning out of the tin. The crownies will keep for 4 or 5 days in an airtight container.

Baileys Cheesecake Brownies

We started making alcohol-based treats for summer festivals and this brownie-cheescake hybrid was the most popular of all. It's easy to see why from the first bite.

BROWNIES
180g unsalted butter, plus
    extra for greasing the tin
180g dark chocolate,
    chopped, or callets
120g plain flour
¼ tsp salt
3 large eggs
180g golden caster sugar
1 tsp vanilla extract

**BAILEYS CHEESECAKE
SWIRL**
150g cream cheese
40g golden caster sugar
1 large egg
2 tbsp Baileys Original
    Irish cream liqueur

22cm square baking tin
    or brownie tin
Baking paper

Makes 12 squares

Preheat the oven to 180°C/160°C fan/gas 4. Grease and line your baking tin with baking paper.

FOR THE BROWNIES
Melt the 180g butter and chocolate together in a bain-marie (or in a heatproof bowl set over a pan of simmering water).

Sift the flour and salt together and set aside.

In a separate bowl, mix together the eggs, sugar and vanilla extract until well combined. Stir in the butter and chocolate mixture until thick and creamy.

Add the flour and stir until combined.

Pour into the prepared tin and set aside.

FOR THE CHEESECAKE SWIRL
In a bowl, beat the cream cheese and sugar together. Mix in the egg. Add the Baileys and stir until all ingredients are well combined. Pour over the chocolate brownie mixture and, using a knife, gently swirl it in.

Bake for 20 minutes or until just set in the middle. Leave to cool in the tin and chill for 1 hour. To serve, cut into 12 squares.

Brownie Ice Cream Sandwiches

Perfect for rounding off a supper or dinner party, these luscious two-in-one treats are sure to wow your guests.

ICE CREAM
100g white chocolate, broken into pieces, or callets
350ml full-fat milk
100g golden caster sugar
4 large egg yolks
350ml whipping cream

BROWNIE LAYERS
180g unsalted butter, plus extra for greasing the tin
180g dark chocolate, chopped, or callets
120g plain flour
45g cocoa powder
¼ tsp salt
3 large eggs
180g golden caster sugar
1 tsp vanilla extract

COATING (optional)
450g dark or milk chocolate, chopped, or callets, melted and tempered (see p.26)

2 x 22cm square baking or brownie tins
Ice-cream maker (optional)
6 wooden lollipop sticks (optional)

Makes 6 ice cream sandwiches

FOR THE ICE CREAM

In a small saucepan, heat the white chocolate and milk together gently, stirring until the mixture is smooth and the chocolate has melted. Remove from the heat and set aside to cool slightly.

Place the sugar and egg yolks in a large bowl and whisk until the mixture turns pale and leaves a trail when the whisk is lifted. Slowly add the milk mixture, stirring with a wooden spoon.

Strain the mixture into a medium-sized saucepan and cook over a low heat for 10–15 minutes, stirring continuously. Once the mixture forms a custard-like consistency and is thick enough to coat the back of a spoon, remove from the heat. Do not allow the mixture to boil as it will curdle.

Leave the mixture to cool for at least 1 hour, stirring occasionally to prevent a skin from forming.

In the meantime whip the cream to soft peaks, and keep in the fridge until ready to use.

If using an ice-cream maker, add the whipped cream in and fold the custard mixture into the cream. Then churn according to the manufacturer's instructions.

Alternatively, freeze the custard, uncovered, in a freezer container for 1 hour, or until it begins to set around the edges. Turn the custard out into a bowl and stir with a whisk until smooth, then fold in the whipped cream. Return to the freezer and freeze for a further 2 hours. To store, put a lid on the container and keep in the freezer until ready to serve.

FOR THE BROWNIE LAYERS
Preheat the oven to 180°C/160°C fan/gas 4. Grease and line your brownie tins with baking paper.

Melt the 180g butter and the dark chocolate together in a bain-marie (or in a heatproof bowl set over a pan of simmering water).

Sift the flour, cocoa powder and salt together and set aside.

In a separate bowl, mix together the eggs, sugar and vanilla extract until well combined. Stir in the butter and chocolate mixture until thick and creamy.

Add the flour and stir until combined.

Divide the mixture equally between the 2 tins, then bake for 12–15 minutes or until the centre is just set. Leave to cool completely in their tins, then refrigerate for at least 30 minutes.

TO ASSEMBLE
Remove the ice cream from the freezer and let it soften slightly for 5–10 minutes.

Spread the ice cream over one of the brownie layers while still in its tin. Remove the second brownie layer from its tin and place on top of the ice cream. Place in the freezer for 20 minutes, then remove and cut into 6 rectangles. Serve immediately, or follow the coating instructions below.

FOR THE COATING (IF USING)
Once you have cut into rectangles, insert a wooden lollipop stick horizontally into the layer of ice cream in each brownie sandwich and, dip the rectangles, one at a time, into the melted chocolate for a delicious chocolate-coated ice-cream treat. Place on baking paper and leave to set.

Marbled Chocolate Cheesecake

Add chocolate decadence to a classic cheesecake –
the marbling effect looks beautiful.

BISCUIT BASE
75g unsalted butter, melted,
   plus extra for greasing
   the tin
200g digestive biscuits
2 tbsp cocoa powder

CHEESECAKE
100g dark chocolate
500g cream cheese
200g golden caster sugar
75ml double cream
1 tsp vanilla extract
3 tbsp cornflour
4 large eggs

22cm spring-form cake tin
Rolling pin (optional)
Baking paper

Serves 12

Preheat the oven to 150°C/130°C/gas 2. Grease and line the base of the cake tin with baking paper.

FOR THE BISCUIT BASE
Crush the biscuits into crumbs either using a food processor or placing them in a plastic bag and breaking them up with a rolling pin.

Mix the crushed biscuits with the 75g melted butter, then mix in the cocoa powder. Press into the bottom of the prepared tin.

FOR THE CHEESECAKE
Melt the chocolate in a bain-marie (or in a heatproof bowl set over a pan of simmering water) until just melted. If there are any small lumps of unmelted chocolate, remove from the heat and stir until melted. Set aside to cool down.

In a large bowl, beat the cream cheese and sugar together. Then add the double cream, vanilla, cornflour and eggs until well mixed.

Pour a third of this mixture into a separate bowl, then mix in the cooled, melted chocolate until fully incorporated.

Pour the plain vanilla mixture over the biscuit base in the tin, spreading it evenly, then spoon blobs of the chocolate mixture over the top. Using a knife, drag the chocolate through the vanilla mixture to create a marbled effect.

Bake for 40–45 minutes until the edges of the cheesecake are firm but the centre is still wobbly. Leave in the oven to cool completely with the door closed.

Baked Chocolate Tart

It may sound like a cliché but this recipe really is heaven. Every time we make it in the bakery we bake any leftover mousse filling in muffin cases, and eat it. It's quite lucky for our waistlines that we don't make it daily.

SWEET SHORTCRUST PASTRY

80g unsalted butter, chilled, plus extra for greasing the tin

140g plain flour, plus extra for dusting the work surface

1 tsp salt

45g icing sugar

2 large egg yolks

CHOCOLATE MOUSSE FILLING

125g dark chocolate, chopped, or callets

60g unsalted butter

50g golden caster sugar

2 large eggs

20cm tart tin
Rolling pin
Baking beans (or dried beans or rice)
Baking paper
Cling film

Serves 8

FOR THE SWEET SHORTCRUST PASTRY

In a medium bowl, sift the flour and salt together. Rub the 140g butter into the flour with your fingertips until the mixture resembles breadcrumbs. Mix in the sugar, then add the egg yolks. Work everything together with a fork, then your hands, wrap in cling film and refrigerate until firm, about 15–20 minutes.

On a floured surface, use a large rolling pin to roll out the pastry to the thickness of a pound coin. Line the tart tin with the rolled-out pastry, then trim off any excess pastry with a knife. Chill the pastry for 20 minutes, or until firm to the touch.

Preheat the oven to 200°C/180°C fan/gas 6.

Cut a piece of baking paper into a circle at least 3cm larger than both the pastry and the tin, so that it's large enough to fill the tin, right up to the edges and slightly up the sides. Place the paper over the pastry, ensuring it goes right into the corners of the tin, then fill with baking beans (or use dried beans or rice).

Blind bake in the oven for 15 minutes or until the sides of the pastry are firm enough to hold up. When the sides of the pastry feel sandy and firm, remove the beans and paper and return the pastry to the oven for a further 5 minutes, or until the rest of the pastry is cooked through, taking care not to overcook.

Once the pastry is golden, remove from the oven and leave to cool.

FOR THE CHOCOLATE MOUSSE FILLING
In a bain-marie (or in a heatproof bowl set over a pan of simmering water), melt the chocolate and butter together.

Once there are just a few lumps of chocolate left, take off the heat and stir until smooth.

Set aside to cool slightly.

In a medium-sized bowl, whisk the sugar and eggs together until white and fluffy, about 5–8 minutes.

Gently pour the melted chocolate into the egg mixture. Mix in slowly, then use a spatula to combine it fully.

Pour the mixture over the blind-baked pastry and return to the oven for 15–18 minutes, or until the sides of the filling are firm and the centre is slightly wobbly. The sides of the filling will have pulled away from the pastry a little once it's ready.

Leave to cool on a wire rack, then remove from the tin when completely cool.

Cut into 8 slices, to serve.

Chocolate Meringues

These meringues are lightly chocolatey and chewy inside. Dust with cocoa powder and cocoa nibs before they go in the oven and then once they are cooked, dip in tempered chocolate for a luxurious finish.

MERINGUES
200g golden caster sugar
3 large egg whites
2 tsp cocoa powder, plus
　extra for dusting
60g cocoa nibs, to decorate

TO FINISH
250g dark or milk chocolate,
　chopped, or callets

Cook's thermometer
　(optional)
Disposable piping bag
　(optional)
3-prong dipping fork
Baking paper

Makes approx. 16 small or
　8 large meringues

Preheat the oven to 110°C/90°C fan/gas ¼. Line 2 baking sheets with baking paper.

FOR THE MERINGUES
Gently heat the sugar in a small heavy-bottomed saucepan for about 8 minutes until it reaches 100°C. Take care not to overheat as lumps can form. Remove from the heat and set aside.

In a bowl, whisk the egg whites until soft peaks form, then add the sugar gradually and continue to whisk until stiff peaks form. Sift the cocoa powder over the top of the meringue mixture, then gently fold it in.

For large meringues, scoop heaped tablespoonfuls of the mixture onto the lined baking sheets, leaving a good space between each meringue. For small ones, transfer the meringue into a piping bag and cut the end off. Pipe about 16 teaspoon-sized meringues onto the baking paper. They will double in size.

Dust cocoa powder over the meringues, then sprinkle with the cocoa nibs.

Bake for 1 hour for small meringues and 2 for large. When the meringues lift off the paper easily, they're ready.

Remove from oven and leave to cool for 20 minutes before transferring onto a wire rack.

TO FINISH
Melt and temper the chocolate, using the method on p.26. Then dip each cooled meringue in the tempered chocolate by hand. Place on baking paper to set.

Chocolate Fondant

This rich, gooey sponge with a melting middle is easy to prepare and needs only a short time in the oven, making it the perfect after-dinner treat.

112g unsalted butter, at
    room temperature, plus
    extra for greasing
Cocoa powder, for dusting
140g dark chocolate (70%)
200g golden caster sugar
1 tsp vanilla extract
3 large eggs, beaten
100g plain flour, sifted

4 dariole moulds

Serves 4

Preheat the oven to 180°C/160°C fan/gas 4.

Grease the dariole moulds with butter, dust with cocoa powder and shake out the excess. Set aside.

Gently melt the 112g butter and the chocolate together in a saucepan. Remove from the heat and stir in the sugar and vanilla. Leave to cool slightly.

When the butter and chocolate has cooled slightly, whisk the beaten egg into the mixture, a little at a time, then fold in the flour until you have a smooth consistency.

Divide the mixture between the moulds until each one is two thirds full. Place the moulds on a baking tray and bake for exactly 12 minutes.

Remove from the oven, run a knife round the edges and tip out onto serving plates.

Serve warm with vanilla ice cream.

Chocolate Shortbread Biscuits

The classic Scottish biscuit is all the more delicious with a crumbly chocolate twist.

125g caster sugar
25g cocoa powder
225g plain flour
pinch salt
175g unsalted butter, chilled
½ tsp vanilla extract
1 large egg

8cm round biscuit cutter
Baking paper
Cling film

Makes approx. 20 biscuits

Preheat oven to 180°C/160° fan/gas 4.

In a bowl mix the sugar, cocoa powder, flour and salt together. Rub the butter into the dry ingredients with your fingertips until fine, sand-like crumbs form.

Add the vanilla and eggs and mix until a stiff dough forms. Wrap in cling film and refrigerate for 15 minutes.

On a lightly floured surface, roll out the dough to 2cm thickness and cut into shapes using the biscuit cutter. Place 5cm apart onto a baking tray lined with baking paper.

Sprinkle with caster sugar and chill for 20 minutes.

Bake for 8–10 minutes or until the surface appears dry. Allow biscuits to cool for a couple of minutes before transferring to a wire rack to cool completely.

Chocolate Pastry Tartlets

You don't often see chocolate pastry but it's delicious with simple fillings such as crème patisserie and fresh berries. This is a flakier and more delicate pastry than usual due to the addition of cocoa powder, so take care when handling it.

CHOCOLATE PASTRY
110g unsalted butter, chilled, plus extra for greasing the tart moulds
170g plain flour, plus extra for dusting the work surface
1 heaped tbsp cocoa powder
50g icing sugar, sifted
1 large egg yolk

CRÈME PATISSERIE FILLING
2 large egg yolks
50g golden caster sugar
1 tbsp plain flour
1 tbsp cornflour, plus 1 tsp
125ml milk
1 tsp vanilla paste
150ml double cream

Raspberries (optional)
Icing sugar, for dusting

16–18 tart moulds (or 1–2 muffin tin/s)
Rolling pin
5cm pastry cutter
Baking beans
Disposable piping bag
Baking paper
Cling film

Makes 16–18 tartlets

Grease 16 tart moulds with butter (or use 1–2 muffin tin/s).

FOR THE CHOCOLATE PASTRY
In a bowl, sift the flour and cocoa powder together. Rub the 110g butter into the flour with your fingertips until the mixture resembles breadcrumbs. Mix in the icing sugar, then add the egg yolk. Work everything together with a fork and then your hands, but don't overwork or the mixture will shrink. Wrap in cling film and refrigerate for 1 hour.

Roll out the pastry on a floured surface. Use a 5cm pastry cutter to cut into rounds, then line the tart moulds. Chill for another 15 minutes.

Preheat the oven to 200°C/180°C fan/gas 6.

When the pastry is chilled, place a small piece of baking paper over each tart mould and fill with baking beans (or use dried beans or rice). Blind bake for 20 minutes. Remove from the oven and leave to cool completely.

FOR THE CRÈME PATISSERIE FILLING
Whisk together the eggs and sugar in a large bowl until pale. Whisk the plain flour and all of the cornflour into the mixture and set aside.

Place the milk and vanilla in a small saucepan and bring to a simmer, stirring frequently. Remove from the heat and leave to cool for 30 seconds.

(*continues overleaf*)

Slowly pour half of the milk into the egg mixture, whisking continuously, then return the mixture to the remaining milk in the pan. Doing it this way prevents the eggs from scrambling.

Bring the mixture back to the boil. Boil the mixture for 3 more minutes then simmer on low heat for 1 minute more, allowing it to thicken, and whisk continuously until smooth.

In the meantime gently whip the cream. Let the milk cool for 15–20 minutes, then fold in the softly whipped cream.

TO DECORATE
Transfer the filling to a piping bag, cut the end off and pipe the filling into the cooled tart shells. Decorate with raspberries, if using, and dust with icing sugar.

Chocolate Molasses Cookies

This recipe was an accidental discovery. We were trying to make a different kind of cookie but it didn't quite come out as expected. However, the result was a pleasant surprise. The molasses in the dark muscovado sugar add a treacle-like taste to the buttery cookies.

145g plain flour
25g cocoa powder
1 tsp bicarbonate of soda
¼ tsp sea salt
150g unsalted butter, at
   room temperature
55g golden caster sugar
165g dark muscovado sugar
1 tsp vanilla extract
50g dark chocolate, chopped

5cm pastry cutter
Cling film
Baking paper

Makes 16 cookies

In a large bowl, sift together the flour, cocoa, bicarbonate of soda and sea salt. Set aside.

In a separate bowl, cream the butter until soft and smooth. Add the sugars and vanilla, and beat until light and fluffy.

Add the flour mixture and blend thoroughly. Mix in the chocolate pieces until they are evenly distributed.

Transfer the dough to a clean, flat surface, divide into 2 equal parts, then roll into logs about 16cm long and wrap in cling film. Refrigerate for a least 1 hour until firm.

Preheat the oven to 190°C/170°C fan/gas 5. Line 2 baking sheets with baking paper.

Cut each log into 8 x 2cm-thick discs, using a sharp knife.

Place the discs on the lined baking sheets, leaving a gap of at least 5cm between each one.

Chill again for 15 minutes, then bake for 8 minutes or until the centres are just firm to the touch. Remove from the oven and transfer to a wire rack to cool completely.

TIP
The longer you chill the dough, the more likely the cookies will hold their shape.

Chocolate Empanadas filled with Dulce De Leche

Empanadas are a Latin American pastry usually stuffed with something savoury. There are also sweet varieties, and here's my version of the Argentinian-inspired treat, which is filled with dulce de leche.

PASTRY
360g plain flour, sifted, plus extra for dusting the work surface
90g cocoa powder
200g golden caster sugar
Pinch of salt
220g unsalted butter, diced
2 large eggs, plus 1 for glazing
60ml milk
65g demerara sugar, for sprinkling

DULCE DE LECHE
500ml milk
200g golden caster sugar
1 tsp vanilla extract
½ tsp bicarbonate of soda

For speed, use a ready-made 450g jar of dulce de leche, as many supermarkets now stock it.

Sieve
Rolling pin
9cm pastry cutter
Cling film
Baking sheet
Baking paper

Makes approx. 30 empanadas

FOR THE PASTRY
In a large bowl, stir together the flour, cocoa powder, caster sugar and salt. Using your fingertips, rub the butter into the flour until the mixture has the texture of fine breadcrumbs.

Add the 2 large eggs and two thirds of the milk, and combine using your hands until a clumpy dough forms. Add the remaining milk if required.

Turn the dough out onto a lightly floured surface and knead for 1 minute.

Form the dough into 2 balls, then flatten them into discs, wrap in cling film, and chill for 30 minutes.

FOR THE DULCE DE LECHE
In a heavy-bottomed pan, heat the milk on a medium-high heat until it comes to a boil. Add the caster sugar and the vanilla, and stir until completely dissolved. Now stir in the bicarbonate of soda and mix well.

Continue to stir, taking care that the milk doesn't rise too much and that it doesn't get burnt on the bottom of the pan.

Turn the heat down to medium. If the milk foams too much, reduce the heat further. The colour of the milk should now be a pale yellow and will get darker as time goes on.

Keep stirring on a medium heat for 1 hour or so, until the milk has reduced and thickened and is much darker in colour.

When the volume has reduced to one third of its original volume and the mixture is a golden-copper colour, it's ready.

Remove from the heat and carefully pass the mixture through a sieve into a medium bowl to filter and remove the foam that developed on top.

Leave to cool. The dulce de leche can be stored in the fridge for up to a month.

TO ASSEMBLE

Line a baking sheet with baking paper. On a lightly floured surface, roll out the dough to the thickness of a pound coin (about 3mm).

Use a 9cm pastry cutter to cut out circles from the pastry.

Put 1 tsp of filling onto one half of each circle, leaving a 1.5cm border. Wet the edges of each circle with a little water, fold the non-filled half of pastry over the filled half and either crimp the edges together or use a fork to mark the edges. These need to be sealed really well or the filling will leak. This dough will be more fragile due to the addition of cocoa powder, so handle gently.

Repeat with the remaining pastries. Beat the remaining egg and brush it over the pastries to give them a lovely shine when baked. Sprinkle the demerara sugar over the top.

Place the empanadas on the lined baking sheet and chill for at least 30 minutes to help them retain their shape and stay sealed.

Meanwhile, preheat the oven to 190°C/170°C fan/gas 5.

TO BAKE

Bake the empanadas for 15–20 minutes, or until golden brown. Turn out onto a wire rack to cool a little. These are best served warm. Take care when handling the cooked empanadas as the dulce de leche may leak out of the pastry, making it very hot and likely to burn.

Chocolate Cinnamon Rolls

There's nothing I love more than the scent of cinnamon when baking – well, apart from the scent of chocolate of course. So put the two together and one of my all-time favourite treats just got better. This dough will take longer to rise than normal as chocolate inhibits yeast growth, but the rolls will be worth the wait.

DOUGH

2 x 7g sachet fast action
  dried yeast
125ml warm water
185ml milk, room temp.
115g unsalted butter,
  softened, plus extra for
  greasing
510g strong white flour, plus
  extra for dusting
150g golden caster sugar
45g cocoa powder
1 tsp salt
1 large egg and 1 egg yolk,
  plus 1 egg yolk for glazing

FILLING

225g unsalted butter,
  softened, plus extra
  for brushing
100g dark chocolate,
  chopped, or callets
165g light muscovado sugar
2 tsp ground cinnamon
100g pecans, coarsely
  chopped and toasted

MAPLE GLAZE

150g milk chocolate,
  chopped, or callets
200ml maple syrup

1 22 x 33cm Swiss roll tin

Makes 24 rolls

To make the dough, stir the yeast into the warm water in a large bowl and leave to stand for 5 minutes.

Add the milk and 115g butter to the bowl. Add one third of the flour and all of the sugar, cocoa, salt, plus the egg and egg yolk. Beat together for 2 minutes until smooth. Add the remaining flour and mix to form a soft dough.

Turn out onto a well-floured surface and knead for about 8–10 minutes, until the dough is smooth and elastic.

Place in a large, greased bowl, turning the dough once to grease the top. Cover with a damp tea towel and leave to prove in a warm place for about 1½ hours, or until the dough has doubled in size.

Meanwhile, lightly grease your baking tin.

When the dough has doubled in size, punch it down to knock the air out, then turn out onto a lightly floured work surface.

Divide the dough in half and roll the first portion into a rectangle measuring 22 x 33cm.

To add the filling, brush the dough with half of the softened butter, then sprinkle evenly with half of the chocolate, followed by half of the sugar, then half of the cinnamon and, finally, half of the nuts. Repeat with the second portion of dough.

(*continues overleaf*)

Starting with the long side of the rectangle, roll up the dough like a Swiss roll. Cut into 6 equal slices. Repeat with the second portion of dough.

Lay the rolls, with the spirals facing up, in the prepared tin. Cover with a damp tea towel and leave to prove for a further 45 minutes.

Preheat the oven to 190°C/170°C fan/ gas 5.

Beat the remaining egg yolk and brush on the tops of the rolls to give them a lovely shine. Bake for 18–20 minutes or until the tops are hard but the middle is springy to the touch.

FOR THE MAPLE GLAZE

While the rolls are baking, prepare the maple glaze. In a heatproof bowl set over a pan of simmering water, melt the dark chocolate. Remove from the heat, then pour in the maple syrup, stirring to combine. Once thickened, drizzle the glaze on the rolls while they are still warm. Serve the rolls warm or transfer to a wire rack to cool completely.

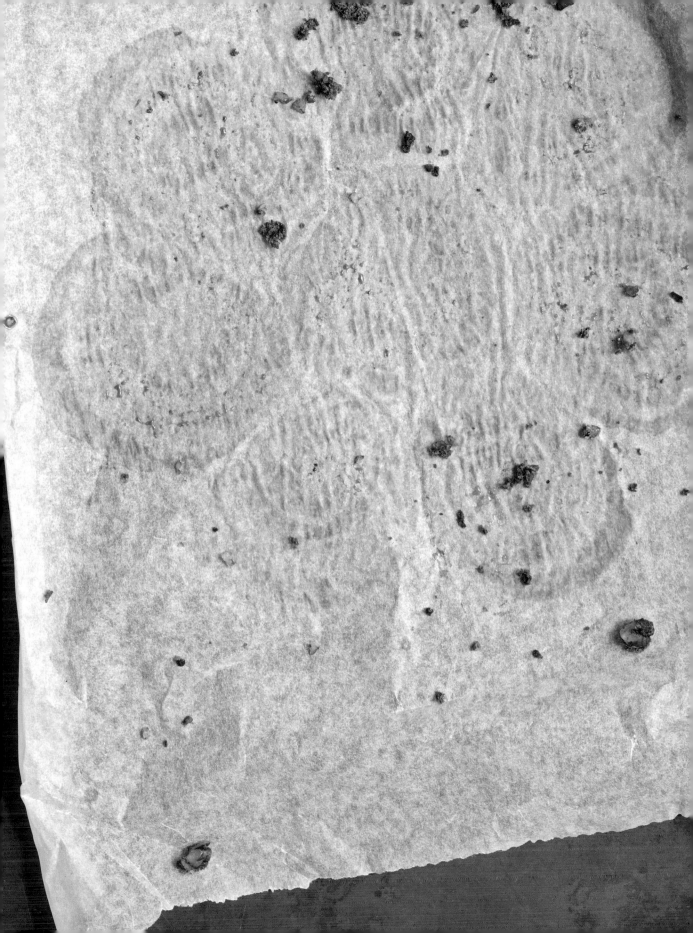

Chocolate Sandwich Biscuits

These are an attractive treat to make for afternoon tea or to give as gifts. Use a variety of cutters to decorate the centres – how about hearts for someone you love, or letters to spell out a name?

COOKIES

125g plain flour, plus extra for dusting the work surface
60g cocoa powder
¼ tsp baking powder
65g dark chocolate, chopped, or callets
¾ teaspoon espresso powder
½ tsp vanilla extract
55g unsalted butter
½ tsp salt
50g golden caster sugar
50g dark muscovado sugar
1 large egg

FILLING

120g mascarpone cheese
250g icing sugar, sifted
1 tsp vanilla extract

5cm pastry cutter
Cutter shapes of your choice (optional)
Cling film
Baking sheets
Baking paper

Makes 12 biscuits sand-wiched together

FOR THE COOKIES

In a medium bowl, sift together the flour, cocoa powder and baking powder. Set aside.

Melt the chocolate in a bain-marie (or in a heatproof bowl set over a pan of simmering water). Remove from the heat and add the espresso powder and vanilla, mixing until incorporated. Leave to cool. Cream the butter, salt and sugars until light and fluffy. Add the egg and mix until combined. Fold in the melted chocolate.

Add the flour a little at a time, mixing well until combined. The mixture will be stiff and crumbly, so remove from the bowl and knead by hand to bring it together.

Form the dough into 2 discs and wrap in cling film. Chill for 15 minutes or until firm.

Preheat the oven to 190°C/170°C fan/gas 5. Line 2 baking sheets with baking paper.

On a well-floured surface, roll out each disc of dough to about the thickness of a pound coin. Cut out 24 biscuit rounds, using a 5cm pastry cutter, and transfer to the lined baking sheets, leaving a 3cm gap between each one. Bake for 8 minutes. Remove from oven and transfer onto a wire rack to cool.

FOR THE FILLING

In a bowl, cream the mascarpone cheese, then gradually add the sugar, mixing well, and stir in the vanilla. Spread a little filling on one of the biscuits, then take a biscuit, place on top and press together firmly. Repeat with the remaining biscuits.

Mille Crêpe Stack

A magnificent-looking cake, and the taller the better. When you cut into it, your guests will be delighted to find a stack of crêpes. Although I must warn you that this ambitious cake is not for the faint-hearted.

CRÊPES
210g unsalted butter, plus extra for cooking the crêpes
555g plain flour
315g golden caster sugar
Pinch of salt
15 large eggs
1.2 litres milk
Zest of 1 orange

HAZELNUT FILLING
500g finely ground hazelnuts
150g golden caster sugar
900g dark chocolate, chopped, or callets
220g unsalted butter, at room temperature
500ml double cream
2 tsp salt

GANACHE GLAZE
Double quantity of recipe on p.48

DECORATION
Toasted or candied hazelnuts
Candied orange peel

Makes 1 stack of about 30 crêpes

Serves 8–10

FOR THE CRÊPES
It's best to make the batter the day before assembling the cake and keep it chilled.

In a small, heavy-bottomed pan, melt the 210g butter until lightly browned, then remove from the heat and set aside.

In a large bowl, sift together the flour, sugar and salt. In a separate bowl, whisk together the eggs, milk and orange zest. Gradually add the milk to the flour mixture.

Slowly add the browned butter and stir in. Pour the batter into an airtight container and refrigerate for several hours or overnight.

When you are ready to cook the crêpes, melt a little butter in a large crêpe pan or small frying pan over a medium heat.

Remove the pan from the heat and pour about 3 tablespoons of the batter into the pan, swirling the pan so the batter covers the base. Reduce the heat to medium-low and return the pan to the heat.

Cook for about 30 seconds until all the edges are golden and the centre is dry. Flip the crêpe over and cook the second side for 30 seconds. Slide the crêpe onto a flat dish or plate.

Repeat until you have about 30 crêpes.

(continues overleaf)

FOR THE HAZELNUT FILLING

In a bowl, mix the ground hazelnuts and caster sugar together until it forms a smooth buttery paste.

Melt the chocolate in a bain-marie (or in a heatproof bowl set over a pan of simmering water). Remove from the heat and whisk in the butter until fully incorporated. Whisk in the cream and salt and then the hazelnut mixture.

Leave the mixture to cool before using.

TO ASSEMBLE THE CRÊPES

Place a crêpe on a cake stand or serving platter. Spread with a thin layer of the hazelnut filling, taking it right to the edges. Top with another crêpe and repeat the process until you have used all the crêpes and hazelnut filling.

Refrigerate for around 15 minutes or until firm.

FOR THE GANACHE GLAZE

Make the ganache, using the recipe on p.48 and doubling the quantities.

Using a palette knife, spread the ganache glaze over the top of the cake and right to the edges. Spread the remaining glaze around the sides of the cake. Refrigerate for 20 minutes until the glaze is set.

Decorate with toasted or candied hazelnuts and candied orange peel.

TIP

It can be tricky to get neat edges around the cake, so if you're a perfectionist like me, once the cake is assembled, cut round the cake with a sharp knife, using the base of a cake tin 2–3cm smaller than your crêpe stack as a guide. Then spread the ganache over the cake.

Chocolate Sticky Toffee Pudding

Chocolate makes this already indulgent British pudding even more wicked. Chocolate and toffee pair so well in this version, which is baked rather than steamed.

85g unsalted butter, softened, plus extra for greasing
200g Medjool dates, stoned and chopped
250ml boiling water
½ tsp bicarbonate of soda
85g dark chocolate, chopped, or callets
150g golden caster sugar
2 large eggs, beaten
180g self-raising flour

CHOCOLATE TOFFEE SAUCE
130g dark muscovado sugar
150ml golden syrup
60g unsalted butter
115ml double cream
50g dark chocolate

20cm square baking tin

Serves 8–10

Preheat the oven to 180°C/160°C fan/gas 4. Grease your baking tin.

Soak the dates in the boiling water in a saucepan and bring to the boil. Reduce to a simmer and cook for 10 minutes to soften the dates. Stir in the bicarbonate of soda.

At the same time melt the chocolate in a bain-marie (or in a heatproof bowl set over a pan of simmering water). In a medium bowl, cream the 85g butter and the sugar together until pale and creamy, then beat in the eggs and melted chocolate. Sift in the flour.

Fold in the date mixture, then pour into the prepared tin.

Bake in the oven for 30–35 minutes, or until the top is just firm to the touch. Turn out onto a wire rack to cool.

FOR THE CHOCOLATE TOFFEE SAUCE
While the pudding is in the oven, make the chocolate toffee sauce.

Place the sugar, golden syrup and butter in a pan and bring slowly to the boil, stirring all the time. Let the mixture bubble for a few minutes, then carefully stir in the cream.

Cook for another 2 or 3 minutes, stirring, or until the sauce is thick, sticky and glossy, then add the 50g chocolate and whisk until fully incorporated.

TO SERVE
Cut the baked pudding into 12 squares and pour the warm chocolate toffee sauce over it.

SEASONAL TREATS

Heart-shaped Chocolate Box Cake

It may seem ambitious but this cake and chocolate combination is easier than you might think. It makes an impressive Valentine's Day gift where you can show off both your chocolate and baking skills. The idea is to use the cake as a chocolate box to showcase your home-made truffles.

125g unsalted butter, softened, plus extra for greasing the tins
50g cocoa powder
75ml boiling water
50ml full-fat milk
115g self-raising flour
1 tsp baking powder
¼ tsp bicarbonate of soda
¼ tsp salt
150g golden caster sugar
2 large eggs
1 tsp vanilla extract

RASPBERRY BUTTERCREAM
50g fresh raspberries
125g unsalted butter, softened
250g icing sugar, sifted
1 tsp vanilla extract
2 tbsp milk

DECORATION
600g dark chocolate, chopped, or callets

Acetate sheets
2 x 25cm heart-shaped cake tins
Baking paper
Cling film

Serves 8–10

Preheat the oven to 180°C/160°C fan/gas 4. Grease and line the cake tins with baking paper.

Put the cocoa powder in a heatproof bowl. Pour the boiling water into the cocoa and stir until smooth. Leave to cool slightly before adding the milk. Stir to combine.

In a medium bowl, sift the flour, baking powder, bicarbonate of soda and salt together. Set aside.

In a separate bowl, cream the 125g butter until light and fluffy. Gradually add the sugar and beat for another 5 minutes. Mix in the vanilla extract.

Add the eggs, one at a time, mixing for 1 minute between each addition.

Gently add half the flour and mix in until just combined, then add half the cocoa mixture. Repeat with the remaining flour and cocoa mixture, then pour evenly into the prepared heart-shaped tins.

Bake for 30 minutes or until a cocktail stick inserted into the centre of one of the cakes comes out clean.

Turn out onto a wire rack to cool completely.

FOR THE BUTTERCREAM
Use a fork to mash the raspberries, then set aside. Beat the butter until smooth and creamy, then add the sugar gradually and beat until light and fluffy. Beat in the vanilla. Add the mashed raspberries and beat until combined. Beat in the milk.

(continues overleaf)

TO ASSEMBLE

Level the cooled cakes with a palette knife. Place one of the cakes on a cake board or stand to form the bottom layer, and spread a thick layer of buttercream over it. Top with the second cake, then spread a thin layer of buttercream over the top and then the sides of the whole cake, covering it completely. This is your crumb coat to be covered in chocolate.

TO DECORATE

Line one of the now empty cake tins with cling film.

Melt and temper the chocolate, using the method on p.26. Pour a third of the melted chocolate evenly into the prepared tin, then tap the tin on a flat surface to remove any air bubbles. Set aside for the chocolate to set.

Once set, carefully remove the chocolate from the tin and place over the top of the layer cake.

For the sides of the cake, cut 2 strips of acetate, each the length of one side of the heart (from the top centre point to the bottom centre point) and about 5cm deeper than the crumb-coated cake. You can use baking paper as a template by tracing round the cake.

Using a palette knife, spread a thick layer of chocolate on one of the strips of acetate, covering the entire surface. Working quickly and with the chocolate facing the cake, position the strip around one side of the cake – from the bottom centre point to the top centre point. Use your hands to smooth it in place. Leave to set, and repeat with the second strip of acetate for the other side of the cake.

Once the chocolate has set, gently peel away the strips of acetate.

You will now have a beautiful chocolate box cake to fill with your home-made truffles or filled chocolates of your choice. This method can also be used for a square or round cake if preferred.

Fondant-filled Easter Eggs

These are great treats to make with kids, and you can mix up the sizes if you wish. This recipe makes enough for 12 small eggs or one large one. The filling is a fun surprise when unsuspecting guests crack into an egg.

FONDANT
200ml golden syrup
100g unsalted butter,
    at room temperature
325g icing sugar, sifted
¼ tsp salt
1 tsp vanilla bean paste
Yellow food colouring paste

COATING
450g plain chocolate,
    chopped, or callets

12-hole chocolate egg mould
    with 5.5cm cups (or
    1 large mould)
2 disposable piping bags

Makes enough for 12 small
    eggs or 1 large egg

FOR THE FONDANT
In a medium bowl, whisk together the golden syrup, butter, sugar, salt and vanilla until well combined.

Place a quarter of the mixture into a small bowl and mix in a tiny amount of food colouring, bit by bit, until you reach the desired colour of an egg yolk.

Refrigerate both mixtures for 30 minutes.

FOR THE COATING
In the meantime, melt and temper the chocolate, using the method on p.26. Fill the egg moulds with the melted chocolate, following the technique for moulded chocolates on p.29 and saving any excess chocolate. Leave to set, then fill the egg moulds with more melted chocolate to give a nice thick shell of chocolate. Leave to set again, then remove the chocolate shells from the moulds. Each chocolate mould will make half an Easter egg shell.

TO ASSEMBLE
Remove the fondant mixtures from the fridge. Spoon the white and yellow mixtures into 2 separate piping bags with the ends snipped off.

Pipe the white fondant into each chocolate shell, filling them to about three quarters of the way up. Now pipe a blob of the yellow mixture into the centre of half of the shells. Leave to set.

Using a hot knife or spatula, warm the outline of one of the shells, then place another shell on top to seal it, making a complete Easter egg. Repeat with the remaining shells.

Halloween Chilli Chocolate Mousse Pots

What better way to thrill your guests at Halloween than with these chilli chocolate mousse pots with a chocolate tombstone to boot. Leave out the chilli if you want and you've still got a fabulous dessert for any time of year.

125g dark chocolate, chopped, or callets
60g unsalted butter
1 tsp chilli paste
50g golden caster sugar
2 large eggs

DECORATION
1 pack Oreos
12 white chocolate wafer thins (see Techniques on p.34)
50g dark chocolate, chopped, or callets

12 small pots or ramekins
Rolling pin (optional)
Disposable piping bag
Baking paper

Makes approx. 12 pots

In a bain-marie (or a heatproof bowl set over a pan of simmering water) melt the chocolate and butter together. Once there are just a few lumps of chocolate left, take off the heat and stir until smooth.

Mix in the chilli paste, then set aside to cool slightly. In a medium bowl whisk the sugar and eggs together until white and fluffy, about 5–8 minutes.

Gently pour the melted chocolate into the egg mixture. Mix in slowly, then use a spatula to combine the chocolate fully.

Spoon the mixture into 12 small pots or ramekins and chill for 2 hours.

TO DECORATE
Crush the Oreos either by placing in a sealable plastic bag and using a rolling pin to mash them, or in a food processor. Pour the crumbs over the top of each mousse pot.

Place the white chocolate wafers on a sheet of baking paper.

Melt the dark chocolate. Transfer to a piping bag with the end snipped off and pipe the initials RIP onto each one. Leave to set.

Insert a wafer about halfway into each pot.

Bûche de Noël

Nothing says Christmas like a traditional yule log. Use this recipe to celebrate the festive season, or leave out the chocolate buttercream and you have a delicious chocolate Swiss roll for all year round.

CAKE
240g dark chocolate
6 large eggs, separated, at
  room temperature
160g golden caster sugar
1 tsp vanilla extract
1 tsp cream of tartar
Butter, for greasing the tin
Flour, for dusting the baking
  paper

WHIPPED CREAM FILLING
250ml whipping cream,
  room temperature
1 tsp vanilla extract
50g icing sugar

CHOCOLATE BUTTERCREAM ICING
75g dark chocolate,
  chopped, or callets
120g unsalted butter, at
  room temperature
250g icing sugar, sifted,
  plus extra for dusting

DECORATION
chocolate holly (optional
  – see overleaf)

1 baking tin measuring
  40 x 30cm
Baking paper

Serves 12–15

Preheat the oven to 180°C/160°C fan/gas 4. Grease and line the baking tin with baking paper. Then grease the paper and dust with flour.

Melt the chocolate in a bain-marie (or in a heatproof bowl set over a pan of simmering water). Remove from the heat and leave to cool.

In a bowl, beat the egg yolks and 50g of the sugar until light and fluffy. Beat in the vanilla. Scrape down the sides of the bowl, then add the melted chocolate and beat until just combined.

In a separate bowl, whisk the egg whites until foamy, then add the cream of tartar and beat until soft peaks form. Gradually beat in the remaining sugar until stiff peaks form.

Fold a small amount of the egg white into the egg yolk mixture, using a spatula. Then fold in the remaining egg white until just incorporated. Don't over-mix or the batter will deflate.

Spread the mixture evenly into the prepared tin. Bake for 15–17 minutes until the cake is puffy, has lost its shine and springs back when lightly pressed with a finger.

Remove from the oven and place on a wire rack to cool in its tin. Cover the cake with a clean, slightly dampened tea towel.

(continues overleaf)

FOR THE WHIPPED CREAM FILLING

Place the whipping cream, vanilla and icing sugar in a large mixing bowl and stir to combine. Whisk until stiff peaks form.

TO ROLL UP

Spread the filling over the cooled cake then gently roll up the cake, working towards you and peeling off the baking paper as you go. Trim a slice off each end of the cake at an angle and set aside, then place the cake, seam side down, on a cake stand or board.

FOR THE CHOCOLATE BUTTERCREAM ICING

Melt the chocolate in a bain-marie (or in a heatproof bowl set over a pan of simmering water), then leave to cool slightly.

In a bowl, beat the butter until light and fluffy. Gradually add the sugar and beat until smooth and combined. Mix in the melted chocolate.

Using a palette knife, spread the buttercream over the cake, then use a fork or palette knife to create a ridged log pattern, and chill until ready to serve. Dust with icing sugar before serving and decorate with chocolate holly if using.

Chocolate Holly

10–12 holly leaves, washed and dried
200g dark chocolate, chopped or callets
edible gold powder (optional)

Paintbrush
Baking paper

To decorate the holly leaves melt and temper the chocolate using the method on p.26. Brush the top of each holly leaf with the chocolate and place on baking paper to set. Once set, gently peel the leaf away from the chocolate. Dust with edible gold powder if you wish.

Boiling Sugar

Some recipes require the boiling of sugar to make caramels, sugar shards, toffee and other confections. If you don't have a sugar thermometer use these guidelines to reach the right boiling temperatures.

When sugar syrups are cooked, the water boils away and the temperature of the sugar increases. The temperature the sugar reaches tells you what it will be like when it cools. The different temperature stages below are named based on this. For each of these you can test your sugar syrup by using a spoon to drop a small amount in a bowl of cold water then checking it to see how soft or firm it is out of the water. Take care when removing the sugar from the water especially when the temperature ranges get higher.

Thread Stage: 102°C–112°C
The sugar syrup forms a liquid thread that will not ball up in the water. This stage makes a sugar syrup.

Soft Ball Stage: 112°C–118°C
The sugar syrup forms a soft, flexible ball which, when removed from the water, will flatten after a few seconds in your hand. This stage makes fudge and praline.

Firm Ball Stage: 118°C–121°C
The sugar syrup forms a firm ball, which won't flatten when removed from the water but remains malleable and only flattens when squeezed. This stage makes caramel.

Hard Ball Stage: 121°C–129°C
Look for thick threads as the sugar drips from a spoon. The syrup will form a hard ball when dropped into cold water and it won't flatten when removed from the water but can still be squashed. This stage makes caramel, nougat and marshmallow.

Soft Crack Stage: 129°C–143°C
Look for small bubbles at the top of the boiling mixture which are thick and close together. The syrup will form flexible threads when dropped into the water, which when removed will bend slightly then break. This stage makes butterscotch and honeycomb.

Hard Crack Stage: 143°C–160°C
The syrup will form hard, brittle threads when dropped in water. This stage makes toffees.

SAFETY
When boiling sugar you want to stop it from crystallising otherwise you'll end up with a very grainy caramel so make sure the pan and utensils are clean and dry. While cooking, keep a pastry brush to hand, dipping it in water and brushing the insides of the pan to prevent sugar crystals forming along the sides. A copper pan is great (but not essential) for caramel as it distributes heat really evenly. Take great care when handling caramels and boiling sugar. Sugar gets extremely hot so take care not to let it splash your skin or clothing when making or pouring it.

Marshmallow Fluff

Use this easy recipe to make the home-made marshmallow fluff used in some of the recipes in this book.

400g golden caster sugar
1 tsp glucose syrup
200ml water
2 large egg whites

Cooks thermometer
   (optional)

Makes approx 300ml

Place the sugar, glucose syrup and the 200ml water in a heavy-bottomed saucepan and bring to the boil. Heat until a thermometer reaches 129° C. Stir thoroughly and brush down any sugar on the sides of the pan with a wet pastry brush.

In a clean, medium-sized mixing bowl, whisk the egg whites until stiff peaks form. Continue to whisk and very slowly pour the sugar syrup into the egg whites. Take care not to let the sugar syrup touch the whisk directly, instead letting it pour down the side of the bowl – this will stop the marshmallow fluff forming crystals. Continue to whisk until the mixture is thick and glossy.

Transfer to a sealable container and store at room temperature until ready to use. The marshmallow fluff will keep for a few days stored in the fridge if the container is airtight.

Suppliers

Below are listed the best suppliers of chocolate making and baking equipment for the home cook as well as brands that I recommend for good quality chocolate.

EQUIPMENT

Home Chocolate Factory
Unit 5, 1,000 North Circular Road, London NW2 7JP
www.homechocolatefactory.com
Great for professional polycarbonate moulds, colourings, flavourings, packaging, cocoa butter, lollipop sticks, acetate, thermometers and all equipment. They also sell Callebaut coverture callets.

Lakeland
Stores nationwide and online
www.lakeland.co.uk
Huge range of quality bakeware and kitchen equipment. They also sell silicone chocolate moulds and lollipop sticks.

Squires Kitchen
www.squires-shop.com
An extensive selection of polycarbonate moulds, equipment and chocolate. They also sell small pots of cocoa butter in sets of different colours.

The Cake Decorating Company
Unit 2b Triumph Road
Nottingham
NG7 2GA
www.thecakedecoratingcompany.co.uk
A one-stop shop for equipment. Stockists of Callebaut chocolate couverture.

CHOCOLATE BRANDS

Callebaut
www.callebaut.com
A good quality and widely available Belgian chocolate couverture. Sold in callets or very large bars in specialist stores or online.

Le Menier
A good quality Swiss chocolate, ideal for baking or melting. Available in the baking section at most large supermarkets. Sold as 100g bars.

Montezuma's
www.montezumas.co.uk
A British brand producing Fairtrade chocolate. They produce 2kg bags of couverture for the home cook.

Green & Black's
www.greenandblacks.com
A British brand producing Fairtrade organic chocolate and my favourite cocoa powder. You can find their bars at most supermarkets.

About the Author

Molly Bakes began her baking career in 2009 when she lost her job in the recession. She is not a formally trained baker so she knows how to take the mystery out of seemingly specialist areas of baking. Her first book *Cake Pops*, published in 2011, was a hit. Her fans have included *Vogue* and Lady Gaga.

Acknowledgements

What a blessing to be asked to do a second book. Thanks to everyone who enjoyed the first one and helped make it a success.

A big thank you to Kimberly and Alice who tested and perfected lots of the recipes in the book. And to the rest of the Molly Bakes team – Tash, Izzy and Tamara – thank you for everything.

As always, thanks to my family and my husband Olly for all the support.

Rowan, once again, thank you for setting me this fantastic challenge – I have learnt so much more about an ingredient I have always loved and it's taken me on an exciting new journey. Thanks also to everyone who worked on the book: Georgia for the beautiful photography, Polly for the wonderful food and prop styling, Fred for the design and to everyone else who has helped make this book special.

INDEX

fruit (dried): Dark Chocolate Fruit
and Nut Slab 106
Fudge, Chocolate & Coffee Double
Decker 118

G
ganache
  as a glaze 48
  flavouring 48
  for truffles 48
  whipped ganache 48

H
Halloween Chilli Chocolate Mousse
  Pots 174
hand-rolled truffles 32
harvesting cocoa beans 12
hazelnuts
  Caramel & Hazelnut Squares 63
  Chocolate Hazelnut Bars 98
Heart-shaped Chocolate Box Cake
  169
Home-made Caramel Nougat Bars 91
honey: Fig, Honey & Walnut
  Chocolates 62
Honeycomb, Crunchy 95
Hot Chocolate, Spanish 122

I
ice cream
  Brownie Ice Cream Sandwiches 140
  Chocolate Praline Ice Cream 125

L
lavender: Orange & Lavender Truffles 76
lemon
  Lemon & Basil Chocolates 54
  White Chocolate Nut Clusters with
    Candied Lemon 85
lychees: Rose & Lychee Chocolates 55

M
Maple Bacon Chocolate Slab 107

Marbled Chocolate Cheesecake 142
marshmallow
  Chocolate Marshmallows 124
  Marshmallow Fluff 179
  Rocky Road 112
Matcha & Pistachio White Chocolate
  Truffles 70
marzipan: Pistachio Marzipan &
  Raspberry Diamonds 60
melting chocolate 26–7
Meringues, Chocolate 146
Mille Crêpe Stack 161
Millionaire's Shortbread 92
mint: Fresh Mint Leaf Chocolates 52
moulded chocolates 29
mousse: Halloween Chilli Chocolate
  Mousse Pots 174

N
nougat
  Chocolate Nougat Fingers 110
  Home-made Caramel Nougat Bars 91
nuts
  Caramel & Hazelnut Squares 63
  Caramel Pecan Clusters 80
  Chocolate Hazelnut Bars 98
  Chocolate Nougat Fingers 110
  Chocolate-Coated Nuts 87
  Dark Brazil Nut Brownies 136
  Dark Chocolate Fruit and Nut Slab 106
  Fig, Honey & Walnut Chocolates 62
  Matcha & Pistachio White Chocolate
    Truffles 70
  Pistachio Marzipan & Raspberry
    Diamonds 60
  Rocky Road 112
  Toffee Popcorn Peanut Clusters 81
  White Chocolate Nut Clusters with
    Candied Lemon 85

O
orange
  Candied Citrus Sticks 79